GREAT AMERICAN
ROAD TRIPS
Best of 50 States

Sunflowers offer a warm welcome to visitors at Iowa's Badger Creek State Recreation Area.

▼
Oak trees planted in the early 19th century line the entrance to Louisiana's Oakland Plantation.

© 2022 RDA Enthusiast Brands, LLC.
1610 N. 2nd St., Suite 102
Milwaukee, WI 53212-3906

ISBN
978-1-62145-844-9 (Hardcover)
978-1-62145-845-6 (Paperback)
978-1-62145-846-3 (E-Pub)

COMPONENT NUMBER
116400110H

We are committed to both the quality of our products and the service we provide to our customers. We value your comments, so please feel free to contact us at *TMBBookTeam@TrustedMediaBrands.com.*

For more *Country* products and information, visit our website: *www.country-magazine.com*

Printed in U.S.A.
1 3 5 7 9 10 8 6 4 2 (Hardcover)
Printed in China
1 3 5 7 9 10 8 6 4 2 (Paperback)

PICTURED ON FRONT COVER
Waitsfield, Vermont,
Mira/Alamy Stock Photo

ILLUSTRATIONS Anna Simmons

ADDITIONAL PHOTO INFORMATION
Pages 6-7: Piedras Blancas Light Station, California
Pages 46-47: Caddo Lake State Park, Texas
Pages 66-67: Indianola, Iowa
Pages 106-107: Sanibel Island, Florida
Pages 148-149: Stonington Harbor, Connecticut

Text, photography and illustrations for *Great American Road Trips: Best of 50 States* are based on articles previously published in *Country* magazine (*www.country-magazine.com*).

CONTENTS

Kenai Fjords ◄ National Park in Alaska is home to a variety of marine animals, including humpback whales, orcas, puffins and sea otters.

▼

Hay bales dot a lush field near New York's Keuka Lake.

PAT & CHUCK BLACKLEY

AMERICA THE BEAUTIFUL

ONE OF THE MOST magical parts of going for a long drive in the United States is watching the country's landscape transform right before your eyes. Each state contains myriad vistas: In Iowa, flat plains give way to rolling hills and rocky bluffs that overlook the coursing Mississippi River. In Arizona, sparse deserts morph into dense mountain forests as the elevation rises. And in Connecticut, you can drive from charming seaside towns to farm country in no time.

Great American Road Trips: Best of 50 States embraces the rich diversity of America's landscapes, landmarks, communities and cultural events by celebrating must-see destinations in every state. From internationally renowned parks and historical sites to small towns, scenic byways and off-the-beaten-path adventures, the trips highlighted here offer something for every kind of traveler.

So whether you're a nature lover, history buff or veteran road warrior, read on for travel stories and photos guaranteed to pique your interest and fuel your wanderlust. The firsthand accounts—organized by region of the country and accompanied by insider tips, nearby attractions and more— will have you feeling inspired to pack your bags and set out on the open road. Just turn the page and get ready for an adventure—50 states and countless memories await.

—FROM THE EDITORS

WEST

Anchorage and Cook Inlet are part of the view from Flattop Mountain in Chugach State Park.

STORY AND PHOTOS BY
JODY OVERSTREET

ROAD TRIPS FROM ANCHORAGE

THESE TRIPS FROM ALASKA'S LARGEST CITY DELIVER ADVENTURE FOR EVERY INTEREST, FROM WATCHING WILDLIFE TO HIKING MOUNTAINS AND GLACIERS.

FROM ANCHORAGE, the breadth and beauty of the wild Alaskan frontier opens up to travelers. Here, I've chronicled just a few of my favorite regional destinations and drives; they are all worth exploring as part of a visit to this magical place.

East of Anchorage lies Chugach State Park, a vast wilderness boasting nearly half a million acres of alpine meadows, rugged peaks, tidal flats and waterfalls. Watchable wildlife is abundant here: moose, bears and lynxes roam freely, mountain goats scale rocky precipices and salmon spawn. Look out for willow ptarmigan, Alaska's state bird.

Nearly 300 miles of maintained trails crisscross the park, with several trails following portions of the Old Iditarod Trail (the segment of the trail outside the park is part of the course for the annual Iditarod Dogsled Race). Hikers of all abilities will find something to enjoy here. While the trails are easily accessible from bustling Anchorage, they tend to remain peaceful even in the busier summer months.

A few hours south of Anchorage, in Homer, summer brings pink-purple fireweed blossoms to the mountain meadows along Skyline Drive. This easy-to-do route has scenic pullouts with views of Kachemak Bay, Cook Inlet and several active volcanoes at a distance. Wonderful hiking trails in this area lead to more views of the colorful fireweed blossoms, so named

FUN FACT

Grizzly bears and brown bears are technically members of the same species. The key difference is their geographic location. Brown bears live in coastal areas and feast primarily on marine resources, while grizzlies live further inland and tend to be smaller.

WORDS TO THE WISE

Come to Alaska prepared for an adventure: Bring good rain gear, warm clothing, sturdy footwear, insect repellent and binoculars.

SIDE TRIP

Denali National Park and Preserve is home to plentiful Alaskan wildlife, as well as Denali itself, the tallest mountain in North America (the peak was once known as Mount McKinley). Note: Campground stays and bus rides should be booked in advance here. *nps.gov/dena*

NEARBY ATTRACTION

The Eagle River Nature Center offers public programs and guided hikes, as well as platforms and trails for wildlife viewing. *ernc.org*

▼

Lake Clark National Park is home to many coastal brown bears.

because they are often the first plants to grow over a burn area.

For another memorable drive from Anchorage, consider heading south to Seward. Seward Highway, which links Anchorage to the historic port city, is a gorgeous 127-mile route that delivers the best of Alaska as it winds through the Chugach Mountains and Kenai Peninsula. The highway gives travelers access to excellent trails and lots of chances to spot local wildlife, including Dall sheep, moose, brown and black bears and bald eagles.

For amazing vistas of the Chugach Mountains en route to Seward, be sure to make a make a stop at Potter Marsh. The convenient parking lot is accessible from the highway on the south side of Anchorage. From a lengthy boardwalk traversing the marsh, summer visitors can watch for migratory birds nesting, moose grazing and salmon swimming to their spawning grounds.

Once you've arrived in Seward, take a day cruise with Major Marine Tours and sail to Kenai Fjords National Park. There you might see humpback whales, orcas, puffins and sea otters. While the park's star attractions are the deep, narrow fjords referenced in its name, this diverse wilderness covers almost 700,000 acres of coastline, mountains and more than 35 named glaciers.

The *Alaska Almanac* estimates that the state has 100,000 glaciers, though only 616 of them are named. Setting foot on one of these towering wonders is an experience like no other. Back in the Chugach Mountains south of Anchorage, I photographed a trio of hikers exploring the blue ice atop Knik Glacier. The awe-inspiring formation is 5 miles wide and calves daily. The hikers were dwarfed by the depth of the cracks on the surface.

If you're eager to see a glacier up close, consider a Glacier Landing trip with Alaska Helicopter Tours, which operates throughout south-central Alaska. The helicopter hovers above the ice, giving visitors a bird's-eye view of the icebergs and crevasses, and then lands on the glacier.

Flightseeing tours are vital for any visitor looking to witness the full extent of this region's natural beauty. Though Alaska is roughly 20% the size of the contiguous United States, it contains only 0.004% (17,735 miles) of its public roads. Plane and helicopter tours allow travelers to see otherwise inaccessible areas. If seeing coastal brown bears in pristine native habitats is on your bucket list, take a fly-out trip (you come back the same day) from Anchorage to Lake Clark National Park.

However you choose to explore this region, Alaska will reward you with wild beauty and epic adventure. ❧

Hikers explore ◄
Knik Glacier.

▼

The Pacific Coast Highway offers impressive views of Big Sur's McWay Falls.

STORY BY
HELEN TRUSZKOWSKI

PACIFIC COAST HIGHWAY

WITH AN AIRSTREAM RV IN TOW, OUR FAMILY TOOK THE SCENIC ROUTE.

A HOLIDAY ON WHEELS is the ultimate escapist fantasy. Who hasn't longed for the opportunity to drop everything, quit the hustle and bustle of the city and take to the open road? When that opportunity came knocking for our family, we answered, towing a gleaming silver Airstream RV along California's iconic Pacific Coast Highway, one of the world's most spectacular roads.

An enduring fixture of American road trips since 1931, the Airstream—in our case, a new one—offered streamlined comfort. No roughing it required! Cue two adults (my husband and me), two dogs (Daisy and Bob) and one kid (Jack) setting off on a classic family vacation.

The iconic highway, stretching from Dana Point in Orange Country to the town of Leggett in northern California, is at its most captivating between Santa Barbara and Monterey. This is the bit of road you might see in movies and auto ads. State Route 1 cleaves to the edge of the American continent like no other road you will ever drive.

Our first destination after hitching up was Santa Barbara, where we stayed the night at El Capitan Canyon. There is no pressure to attempt anything too adventurous here—borrow a cruiser bike, go for a swim or take a stroll to El Capitan State Beach. We toasted s'mores as the sun set and then stared at the stars and savored the evening's glorious silence.

The next day, we hooked up the RV at the Pismo Coast Village RV Resort. It may sound easy, but it took us newbies four attempts to succeed. Thankfully RV-ing attracts instant community, and a neighbor took pity on us. We hung on his every word.

Strolling into Pismo brought back wonderful memories of a time when family vacations meant stripped-down pleasures. We watched the sunset melt into the ocean like a scoop of orange

NOT TO BE MISSED

Monterey cypresses, gnarled by the wind and ocean spray, are among the highlights you can spot from 17-Mile Drive, a scenic toll road that loops through part of the Monterey Peninsula. Other roadside delights include opulent mansions, rocky headlands and—of course—the Pacific Ocean. *pebblebeach.com /17-mile-drive*

WORDS TO THE WISE

Some areas of the Pacific Coast Highway are susceptible to mudslides. Before traveling to the area, check for closures at *dot.ca.gov*.

NEARBY ATTRACTION

Officially known as Hearst San Simeon State Historical Monument, Hearst Castle was built by publisher William Randolph Hearst on a hill overlooking the coast. The palatial estate took nearly 30 years to complete and contains a museum-quality collection of art to complement the Mediterranean Revival architecture. *hearstcastle.org*

▼

Helen's son, Jack, takes in the coastline's natural beauty.

sherbet, then bounced into our beds like kids on a sleepover.

We packed up the next morning and soared on. At Morro Bay, we wended our way through acres of soft green farmland studded with cabbages and cows. Along a side road we stumbled upon the cute town of Cambria. Here cafes, old-fashioned candy shops and mom-and-pop novelty stores line Main Street (aptly named, since it's the one road that snakes its way through the East and West villages).

The map told us that Cambria is home to Moonstone Beach, so we hustled the dogs down the shaky wooden stairs to the surf below to hunt for the beautiful translucent stones that give the beach its name.

Beyond Cambria, the landscape is stunning, wild and dry, with red-tailed hawks wheeling in the pale blue sky. We pulled in at the Piedras Blancas Elephant Seal Rookery and heard the huge seals long before we saw them.

From Piedras Blancas heading north, the road skirts sheer cliffs alive with wild sage, lavender and thyme, plumes of blue lupines and orange poppies. As we approached Big Sur, the drive became more daunting. Towing an RV along the curvy two-lane road, with the Santa Lucia Mountains and the Pacific Coast on either side of you, is a lot like riding a slow-motion roller coaster. The scenery doesn't whiz by in a blur here but instead looms larger and more breathtaking 'round every bend.

We continue on to Monterey, once the capital of Spanish California. The city is understated and calm. At its north end is the Monterey Bay Aquarium, which houses almost all of the bay's marine life—from a three-story kelp forest to cuddly sea otters and graceful jellyfish. We pet the bat rays and ogle the sharks for hours, breaking away for one last sunset stroll on the secluded sands at Marina Dunes Preserve.

The route home is a straight drive on Interstate 5. I find myself loath to leave my trusty home away from home—we are (quite literally) attached. I'm now completely sold on the RV experience. A blast from the past fit for a modern road trip? Count me in. ◗

HELEN TRUSZKOWSKI

Colorado

STORY BY
JOSHUA BERMAN

PEAK TO PEAK SCENIC BYWAY

JAW-DROPPING VISTAS APPEAR AS THIS COLORADO BYWAY
RISES INTO THE MOUNTAINS.

THIS ICONIC COLORADO DRIVE offers majestic views of snowcapped peaks, chances to spot local wildlife, and quaint mountain towns well worth a visit. The Peak to Peak Scenic Byway, which begins in Central City, 38 miles west of Denver, winds north along the Continental Divide for 55 miles, stringing together routes 7, 72 and 119 into a journey you will never forget. It's my go-to drive when I want to impress visitors or just make some beautiful turns in my car.

I recently popped onto the byway for a relaxed daytrip with my daughters Shanti and Sky. Our first stop was in Nederland, a scenic mountain town with a population of about 1,500 and an elevation of 8,233 feet. "Ned," as it's affectionately known, straddles the byway at Barker Reservoir at the top of Boulder Canyon. Many drivers begin or end their journey here. During the winter, this is the gateway to Eldora Mountain Resort, a small ski area favored by locals. The rest of the year, Nederland is worth a stop for a meal and a beverage, ideally consumed while

The majestic Longs Peak looms over Estes Park.

Points of INTEREST

REST STOPS

At Crosscut Pizzeria and Taphouse in central Nederland, the outdoor patio is an ideal place to watch the creek and the world go by—over salads and pizzas, with craft beer on tap. *crosscutpizza.com*

Peaceful Valley Campground is one of the most popular campgrounds on the Peak to Peak, with 17 sites and access to the Buchanan Pass Trail. *reserveamerica.com*

FUN FACT

The Stanley Hotel in Estes Park is home to one of the state's largest whiskey collections and served as the inspiration for Stephen King's novel and movie *The Shining*. *stanleyhotel.com*

NEARBY ATTRACTION

The Carousel of Happiness is one of Colorado's most whimsical attractions. It opened in 2010, created by local resident Scott Harrison, a Vietnam veteran who spent 26 years handcarving the 50 animals. *carouselofhappiness .org*

▼

Estes Park is a prime place to view elk, particularly during fall.

sitting above the rushing creek and admiring the sublime views.

During hot summers we crave cooler temperatures, which you immediately notice in Nederland. It's easy to spend more time in town than you'd planned, browsing Nature's Own rock shop or the Mining Museum. On this day, we began with a visit to the Carousel of Happiness and then savored coffee and snacks at The Train Cars Coffee and Yogurt Co.

Finally, eager to get my crew on the trail, we grabbed to-go sandwiches at New Moon Bakery and Cafe, piled back into the car and followed the byway just a few miles north to the turnoff to Mud Lake, a lovely forest reflecting pool. We

picnicked there before taking a little stroll in the woods. This fun adventure around Mud Lake was short, easy and laid-back, though longer loops are available too.

The Peak to Peak's claim to fame is sheer altitude. The road actually tops out at 9,300 feet above sea level at its highest point. As you drive north out of Ned, the rising road provides even closer views of the Continental Divide— the windblown crest of the Rockies in all its exposed, beautiful, above-the-treeline glory. After admiring the rock and alpine tundra, lower your gaze to the trees—notably the aspens—which you'll see in abundance on this next stretch toward Ward. In the fall, these pockets of trees are ablaze in amazing yellow hues; luckily, there are several stretches of safe shoulder areas where you can pull off the road and gawk all you want. Be sure to grab your camera.

We soon passed the marked entrance to the Brainard Lake Recreation Area, a high-elevation access point to the Indian Peaks Wilderness that sits at 10,500 feet. We often come to Brainard to snowshoe in the winter or to walk around the lake (a good spot for trout fishing) in the summer. On this day, however, we drove on, passing the tiny towns of Ward and Allenspark and then pulling over at another vista point in front of the unmistakable Camp St. Malo's Chapel on the Rock.

Here you'll find one of the best views of Longs Peak, with a stone church in the foreground. Longs Peak is a "14er," a mountain more than 14,000 feet above sea level (there are 58 of these 14ers in Colorado). The impressive peak, which people have used as a navigation tool for thousands of years, is actually in Rocky Mountain National Park. Here the eastern border of the park comes close to the highway.

The mountains continually amaze as the Peak to Peak twists and turns toward its terminus in Estes Park, home to the Stanley Hotel (built by F.O. Stanley, of Stanley Steamer fame). The hotel's impressive white edifice appears above the road as you enter town. Estes Park is an old-school gateway town—Rocky Mountain National Park is just up the road—so there are many locally owned restaurants, cafes, shops and more worth visiting. Check the Estes Park website, *visitestespark.com*, for information about local attractions, a calendar of upcoming events and current travel conditions.

We ended our journey this time around by grabbing some ice cream and sitting near the creek, enjoying the bliss of another beautiful day as the cold water rushed by. ◗

▼
Autumn brings vibrant color to the area around Brainard Lake.

STORY AND PHOTOS BY
STEPHANIE GONZALEZ

VOLCANOES NATIONAL PARK

SPEND A WEEK EXPLORING CAVES AND TRAILS FORGED BY THE FORCES OF NATURE.

AS PART OF a Marine Corps family, I've visited many incredible places in my life. Hawaii Volcanoes National Park is high up on my list of all-time favorites.

Established in 1916, the park is home to two active volcanoes, Kilauea and Mauna Loa. It covers 335,259 acres of diverse ecosystems, ranging from lush tropical rainforests to the arid Ka'u Desert, so be prepared for all types of weather: hot, dry, wet, windy and cold.

Start your visit at the Kilauea Visitor Center, where the rangers will share stories about past eruptions, some of which truly changed the face of the park. Kilauea's 2020 eruption created a vast lava lake inside the previously drained Halema'uma'u crater.

Next, get ready to walk: We logged an average of 12,000 steps per day, much to the irritation of my kids. But every step was worth it, especially the ones we took along the Kilauea Iki trail! This 4-mile round-trip hike leads to a solid lake of lava created by a 1959 eruption.

The trail begins with a sweeping view of the crater and then descends into a beautiful rainforest. The walk down skirted the edge of the caldera, and we slowly made our way to the floor. It was surprisingly cold on the lava bed and a little tricky to find our footing. We were tempted to take home volcanic rocks, but legend has it that Pele, the local goddess of volcanoes, will curse those who do. We stuck with photos instead.

We also snapped many photos of the Pu'u Loa Petroglyphs, a sacred site that holds more than 23,000 images carved in hardened lava. The trail there was 1.4 miles round trip over very uneven terrain; it was quite slow going, but the glyphs were amazing.

We ended most of our evenings at the Jaggar Museum observation platform overlooking the Kilauea caldera, which spans 2.5 miles and drops 400 feet. We could see magma bubbling up from the surface and numerous stars above—a magical way to end a magical week. ●

Top: Kilauea Volcano has erupted 34 times since 1952. Bottom: Experience the Holei Sea Arch before this 90-foot-high, 550-year-old lava rock formation crumbles into the sea.

Points of INTEREST

REST STOP

Fuel up for your day with breakfast at The Rim at Volcano House. True to its name, this hotel eatery is situated at the edge of the Kilauea caldera and offers incredible views of the volcano through floor-to-ceiling windows. *hawaiivolcanohouse .com*

NOT TO BE MISSED

Nahuku, also known as the Thurston Lava Tube, is an incredible day hike. The 500-year-old lava tube, discovered in 1913, is massive: 600 feet long with a ceiling height of more than 20 feet in places. Parking is limited here, so plan to visit early in the morning or later in the afternoon.

WORDS TO THE WISE

At the summit of Kilauea, the steam vent and sulfur bank sites are easy to visit together. See vapor rise through cracks along the caldera's edge, and smell volcanic gases rich in sulfur dioxide and hydrogen sulfide as they seep out of the ground. Be aware: The gas does smells like rotten eggs.

STORY BY
CONNIE J. THOMPSON

CITY OF ROCKS

THE EERIE LANDSCAPE OF THIS NATIONAL RESERVE ATTRACTS CLIMBERS AND SIGHTSEERS ALIKE.

A SOFT BREEZE welcomes my husband, Kurt, and me as we pull into Albion, Idaho, on our way to the City of Rocks National Reserve. I'm anxious to see this collection of dramatic granite rock formations, called the Silent City by those emigrating on the California Trail during the great gold rush years.

It's a hot morning, and I need a cold drink. Around the next bend, I spot a pink food truck with a flying pig on the side: PiggySue Bar-B-Que. We order Cokes, but the smell of barbecue has me wishing it was closer to lunchtime. Refreshed, we continue on our way.

Entering the town of Almo, we pop into the Tracy General Store. Built in 1894 by William and Harry Eames, the store is currently owned by Kent and Janis Durfee, who boast that this general store is the oldest operating mercantile in Idaho.

Once inside, Kurt looks over the antiques. I head for the deli, where Janis is making sandwiches on fresh homemade bread. Janis is a people person—someone who makes you think you're in your mother's kitchen. As we talk, a basket of cookies catches my eye. I pick up a giant salted-caramel cookie. I'm told that every year 6,000 of these delights find their way into the bags of visitors who come from all over the world to experience City of Rocks.

We continue on our journey into the reserve and remark that the steeple-like rock formations really do look like a city. Soon the road transports us back in time. In the mid-1800s, approximately 240,000 pioneers traveled through City of Rocks on the California Trail. Smooth boulders display the fading signatures of travelers who camped here, and the haunting remnants of homesteads dot the landscape.

The reserve is popular among rock climbers, and as brave souls inch their way up massive granite cliffs, I put my fear aside and scale a much smaller boulder. The view is still incredible!

When it's time to go home, I let out a big yawn and lean sleepily against the door of our truck. I dream of pioneers, cookies and a city made of rocks. •

▼

Granite monoliths and evergreen trees form the skyline of this city.

Points of INTEREST

REST STOPS

City of Rocks is in a remote area, so pick up lunch or snacks and bottled water at Tracy General Store before exploring. You can also stock up on penny candy, Italian soda and ice cream at this old-fashioned mercantile. *tracy -general-store .business.site*

With room names such as Tombstone, Durango and Buffalo Bill, the Almo Inn is a nod to the Old West in decor and spirit, but it's updated with modern amenities including free Wi-Fi and air conditioning. It's also within easy walking distance of the reserve entrance. *almoinn.com*

WORDS TO THE WISE

If you're in the mood for a short, easy hike, take the Window Arch, Bath Rock or Creekside Towers trail. If something more strenuous appeals, try the Flaming Rock or North Fork Circle Creek trail. The 1.2-mile Geological Interpretive Trail has 12 stations that explain the unique granite formations and the forces that shaped them.

Viewing the Garden Wall Trail from across Grinnell Lake shows just how striking (and daunting) the path really is.

Montana

STORY AND PHOTOS BY
JOE DEAN

GLACIER NATIONAL PARK

THIS MAJESTIC PARK HOLDS CHALLENGES, WONDER AND UNEXPECTED CONNECTIONS FOR ONE INTREPID HIKER.

WHEN I SAW the summit of the trail for the first time, I cried. It was a very stressful period of time—both for me personally and for my country. It was 2013, I was midcareer with four quickly growing teenagers, I had recently lost my father to Alzheimer's disease and America was embroiled in a seemingly endless conflict with Afghanistan.

I needed solace, so I had embarked on a mind-stretching, perspective-building and joyful adventure—a solo trip deep into pristine Glacier National Park in Montana. The park, which conserves 1 million acres of peaks and valleys, phenomenal forests and turquoise rivers and lakes, has welcomed more than 100 million visitors since 1911.

I challenged myself to complete an exhilarating hike: the Highline Loop Trail. Its name is a bit of a misnomer, however, as it is a one-way 11.8-mile trail. It's rated "strenuous"—and that's putting it mildly. I also had a weird but decidedly wonderful idea that any trail

worth doing is worth seeing from both directions, so my trip out and back would be a total of 23.6 grueling miles.

About 400 yards from the start of the Highline Loop, hikers encounter a famous ledge with knee-knocking yet spectacular views. For anyone with a fear of heights, this is simply terrifying. Still, the brief section is quite doable (I witnessed children and families of all types traverse this section), even though in many places the ledge is only 6 to 8 feet wide (and feels even narrower). The drop-offs are 100 feet or more, but thankfully they continue for only a few hundred yards. A hand cable makes this section much more manageable.

About 7 miles into the hike, I reached the optional Garden Wall Trail. Many people choose to forgo this side trail, which climbs a muscle-bending 900 feet in just under 1 mile. It ends at an even higher point than the main trail—the top of the Continental Divide, revealing

Points of INTEREST

WORDS TO THE WISE

Glacier National Park has a large grizzly bear population. Carry bear spray and make noise as you hike. If you encounter mountain goats or bighorn sheep, leave them alone; they can become aggressive when provoked.

SIDE TRIP

The 18,500-acre National Bison Range, established in 1908 to protect America's decimated bison population, is now home to 350 to 500 of these iconic animals. Take one of two self-guided auto tours through the range and watch for the bison as well as for elk, black bears, mule deer, antelopes and many birds. *bisonrange.org*

NEARBY ATTRACTION

The Museum of the Plains Indian features a superb collection of costumes, weapons, ceremonial objects and more, as well as dioramas that detail the lifestyles of 11 tribes of the northern Plains before the arrival of white settlers in the 1800s. *doi.gov/iacb /museum-plains -indian*

▼

Joe was so moved by this hike that he repeated it with his son, Sam.

an indescribable view of the Grinnell and Salamander glaciers. Even though this trail is optional and steep, I decided to go for it. Onward to the summit!

Right after I had made up my mind, a young man passed me on the trail. We traded pleasantries and then started walking together. When I asked where he was from, he replied, "Afghanistan." We quickly struck up a friendship as we hiked toward the top together. As I reached the final grueling 10 feet of vertical climb, plugging away on all fours, my new friend turned back to me and extended his hand. We clasped forearms as he pulled me right up to the summit.

I lay down and pulled myself over the crest, supported by this majestic and ancient mountain. A rush of cold air, coming off of the glaciers 1,000 feet below, blew into my lungs, taking my breath away. I suddenly became aware that tears were running down my face.

It was simply one of the most beautiful and incredible sights I had ever seen. I was overwhelmed with gratitude that I was in that place at that time.

There is much about this hike and day that I still remember today. Mostly I remember the view, and I remember my Afghan pal helping me reach this summit, extending his helpful hand, saying, "Here ya go, brother." Ancient forces were at work in that moment. We stood in brotherhood—something that is just easier in the grandeur and scale of nature.

After making my way back to the main trail, I ran into an older married couple from Germany. Having once taught school in Stuttgart, I struck up a conversation in German with them. They looked up the first part of the Garden Wall Trail, undecided, then asked me in perfect English, "Is it worth the climb?"

"*Völlig!*" (absolutely), I replied. ●

▼
Encountering wildlife is fairly common when hiking the Highline.

▼

A hiker treks the 43-mile Ruby Crest Trail through the Ruby Mountains.

STORY BY
CYNTHIA DELANEY

LAMOILLE CANYON

THIS GEM OF A DRIVE THROUGH THE RUBY MOUNTAINS REVEALS SCENIC TREASURES AT EVERY TURN.

SOME DAYS ARE DIAMONDS, some days are stone. Those words, famously sung by John Denver, are ones to live by for most aspects of life. But there are still realms where gems and rocks coexist.

Lamoille Canyon, in northeastern Nevada's Ruby Mountains, is one such oasis. Settlers once assumed the red stones they found in Lamoille Creek were rubies, earning the mountains their name. In reality, the gems were garnets—a brilliant treasure, but worth far less.

Lamoille Canyon Scenic Byway, one of just a few roadways that lead into the mountains, is only 12 miles long, but this short journey really packs a punch. Beginning at the valley floor, at a mere 5,889 feet, the paved road snakes steadily upward to its ending point at 8,784 feet. The breathtaking ride reveals extreme glaciation and peaks that rise to 11,387 feet.

The Ruby Mountains are frequently compared to the Swiss Alps for their

rugged Ice Age sculpting. They've also been called the Yosemite of Nevada for their U-shaped canyons, hanging valleys and gushing waterfalls.

Very soon after the turnoff onto the byway, you'll begin to see the landscape transition from high desert—a sea of sage and grasses—to aspen-, mesquite- and pine-dotted foothills rising up from Lamoille Creek. This area is just one part of the 6.3-million-acre Humboldt Toiyabe National Forest, the largest forest in the Lower 48.

The byway's first stop is the Power House Picnic Area—look for it on the right just after you enter the canyon. Tall white-trunked "quakies" (aspen trees) lushly shade the popular picnic spot. Lamoille Creek runs through this scenic area, and park benches offer a welcome respite from the warmer lowlands in summer.

Just above the picnic area there's a convenient pull-off. In early summer, the wet meadow below is colorfully

Points of INTEREST

REST STOP

Lamoille (pop. 276) is a small hamlet near the base of the Rubies. Pioneers settled the valley in 1865, ranching in the lower reaches. Weary travelers can enjoy two restaurants and one small hotel.

NOT TO BE MISSED

A tour down Lamoille's side roads leads to the picturesque Little Church of the Crossroads. This historic Presbyterian sanctuary was first dedicated in 1905. Braced against a backdrop of a rising range, this building is probably the area's most photographed. *littlechurchofthe crossroads.org*

NEARBY ATTRACTION

The town of Elko is peak cowboy country and is best known for its annual celebration of buckaroo poetry with the National Cowboy Poetry Gathering. Elko has recently become a haven for artistic expression; the town is dotted with murals and a collection of large-scale cowboy boot sculptures— perfect for selfies. *exploreelko.com*

▼
Take a moment to enjoy the view at Liberty Lake.

covered in wild irises, wild geraniums and yellow balsamroot flowers. It's a beautiful sight to behold.

Talbot, the first trail just to the left of the meadow area, is part of a work in progress. It will eventually complete the Secret–Lamoille Trail, a path that will link two canyons. About 4.1 miles of the trail are currently accessible. The climb starts at 6,300 feet, offering views into Lamoille Valley and the rising slopes of the Ruby Mountains. This trail has the lowest elevation of those accessible from the road, making it a popular destination most of the year for exploration on foot or via horseback or snowshoe.

A level stopping point about midway often yields brilliant sunsets, with vivid colors ranging from cotton candy pink to deep plum, laced with wispy clouds and twinges of tangerine and lemon.

Another easy path off this stretch of the byway is the Nature Trail. This short loop includes worthwhile views of a beaver pond, whispering aspens and the southwestern slopes.

Island Lake Trail, near the end of the drive, is a flower lover's dream. From the end of June through July, a bounty of gorgeous blossoms grows along the steadily ascending path. You might find Indian paintbrush, columbine, scarlet gilia and much more. The trail, which is only about 2.9 miles long, is a series of swift switchbacks, but the reward at the top is worth the sweat. Island Lake provides an inspirational alcove at the bottom of a glacial cirque. The water may beckon you, but it is colder than you think!

Ruby Crest Trail begins at the end of the byway. This is no afternoon jaunt. The route stretches 43 miles across highland terrain around a string of lakes. For a day hike, take a shorter version of the main path to Lamoille Lake, roughly 3.7 miles. Along the way, pass by the Dollar Lakes, small ponds left by receding snow.

The entire drive is a scenic lookout, with seriously steep terrain rising in all directions. One casualty from this adventure may be a sore neck—your muscles can get tired from trying to take in every beautiful view!

Along the way, keep an eye out for gray or beige (depending on the season) mule deer. They are often seen along the roadside grazing on wild grasses. Lucky visitors might even get the chance to see a few mountain goats (a species introduced to the area) or Rocky Mountain elk. Rocky Mountain bighorn sheep—aptly named for their impressive curled horns—are another introduced species also sometimes seen alongside or above the road. Golden-mantled ground squirrels, comical yellow-bellied marmots, jack rabbits and other rodents could also make an appearance as you drive the road and take in the sublime beauty around you.

Glacier Overlook, located midway up the canyon, offers visitors an eye-popping view that demands a stop at the pullout. Gazing out from here at the vista before you is like looking back in time: A giant gap in the mountains was carved more than 250,000 years ago by ice, snow and rock as they froze, warmed and descended.

Unfortunately, the 2018 Range Two Fire burned most of the buildings and many trees in the area. Perseverant northern Nevadans, in love with the location, have been rebuilding with a great deal of local support.

The turnaround at road's end offers the opportunity for another spectacular sight. Park the car, step out into the parking area and turn to the north. If this jaw-dropping perspective does not impress you, nothing will. ❧

▼

Daisies bloom along Lamoille Creek.

▼

Colorful remnants of volcanic ash tint the Painted Hills.

STORY AND PHOTOS BY
DAVID JENSEN

JOHN DAY FOSSIL BEDS

THE STUNNING LANDSCAPE OF OREGON'S JOHN DAY FOSSIL BEDS SHEDS LIGHT ON THE EARTH'S ANCIENT PAST.

EARTH PRESERVES its past in layers, piling new atop old like the pages in a history book until the first chapters lie deep beneath the surface. But occasionally, a fortuitous combination of seismic upheaval and massive erosion brings these long-hidden secrets back to the surface and into the light.

The basin of the John Day River in central Oregon is one of those rare places, providing a wondrous glimpse into the plants, animals, climate and geography of an ancient world. These fossil beds sprawl across 10,000 square miles of arid, juniper-dotted hills, canyons and badlands.

While most of this land is privately owned, John Day Fossil Beds National Monument protects 14,000 acres of the area's most spectacular formations in three sites. You can visit all three in a day, but plan to spend much more time there if you aim to really understand what you're seeing.

To make my visit to this intellectually challenging park easier to comprehend, I decided to proceed through the sites in chronological order.

The Clarno Unit features the earliest fossils. Here, you'll find 44-million-year-old evidence of volcanic activity that began to preserve one of the world's most complete and continuous fossil records of the Cenozoic Era, a time also known as the Age of Mammals. The Cenozoic began about 65 million years ago, when something—possibly an asteroid—killed off the planet's dinosaurs and made way for the likes of us to flourish.

Clarno, near the town of Fossil, is the northernmost of the three units. Its castellated cliffs are composed of volcanic mudflows that have entombed everything from brontotheres (ancient mammals that resembled rhinoceroses) to more than a dozen kinds of ancient horses, along with banana, avocado and palm trees.

My second stop is the Painted Hills Unit, which is the most-photographed site in the area. To get there, I drive about 75 miles south from Clarno via a succession of back roads that wind through the desert. About 39 million years ago, more distant volcanoes began depositing ash on top of the Clarno formation.

At Painted Hills, five easily accessible and self-guiding interpretive trails wind

Points of INTEREST

REST STOPS

Some great places to eat in John Day country include the Little Pine Cafe in the town of Mitchell, where you can get burgers in a Western saloon setting; the Snaffle Bit Dinner House in the town of John Day; and the 112-year-old Oxbow Restaurant & Saloon in Prairie City.

The century-old Hotel Prairie in Prairie City offers sweeping views of ranch lands and the snowy Strawberry Mountain Range. *hotelprairie.com*

SIDE TRIP

John Day River is the longest undammed river in the Pacific Northwest. It's a popular rafting and canoeing destination known for stunning scenery and a few moderately challenging rapids. You can rent rafts and canoes or book multiday guided tours.

NEARBY ATTRACTION

The fascinating Kam Wah Chung State Heritage Site commemorates the role of Chinese pioneers in the region. *stateparks .oregon.gov*

▼

The Painted Cove Trail boardwalk meanders through vibrant hills.

through breathtaking landscapes that look like paintings whose colors have begun to run. Leaf Hill Trail displays some of the thousands of leaf fossils discovered here that prompted intense scientific studies in the 1920s and again in the 1990s.

Finally, after another hour of driving to the east, I arrive at the Sheep Rock Unit, home to the area's youngest rocks and the Thomas Condon Paleontology Center. The site is famous for striking blue-green rock beds that were once volcanic ash. Some young deposits of light-colored ash rained from volcanoes as recently as 6 million years ago.

The Sheep Rock Unit also features interesting fossil exhibits, exceptional naturalists and extensive hiking trails. While checking out the visitors center, I discover a paradox: Working with fossils is an urgent business. Fossils

that have lain undisturbed for millions of years can be destroyed in a matter of months once erosion has exposed them to the elements. So scientists here work against the clock to keep weathering from destroying the emerging fossil records forever.

Through it all runs the John Day River—the excavator and architect of this otherworldly scenery. Five million years ago, the rate of erosion began to exceed the rate of deposition, and the river began unearthing the fossilized treasures buried over the previous 40 million years.

Wherever a river has opened up the book of the past, there is much to be learned. Thanks to John Day Fossil Beds National Monument, this part of the country is a fantastic place for anyone with the slightest curiosity about how our world came to be. ◗

Utah

STORY AND PHOTOS BY
TIM FITZHARRIS

SCENIC BYWAY 12

YOU COULD MAKE THIS UNFORGETTABLE DRIVE IN THREE EASY HOURS—BUT YOU SHOULDN'T.

UTAH'S SCENIC BYWAY 12 runs between two of America's most spectacular national parks—Bryce Canyon and Capitol Reef.

On the road's western end, renowned Bryce Canyon National Park features vast amphitheaters of delicately eroded limestone formations tinted in striking shades of pink, orange and red.

The rim of the Paunsaugunt Plateau offers great overlooks and panoramic views that can stretch nearly 200 miles when the air is clear. And don't pass up the chance to hike the trails winding through the slot canyons, windows, fins and spires (called hoodoos). You will never forget the experience.

A couple of miles from the eastern end of the byway, Capitol Reef National Park offers a completely different—but equally awesome—example of nature's rock-carving talents. The park's main feature is shaped by the Waterpocket

▼
Photogenic Sunset Arch is accessible via Hole-in-the-Rock Road.

Points of INTEREST

REST STOP

In the 1880s, Mormon settlers in the Capitol Reef area established Fruita, a community named after its abundant orchards. During the picking season, visitors are welcome to pick their own fruit in the historical orchards, located about a mile from the visitors center. After you're done, reward yourself with a slice of locally baked fruit pie at Gifford Homestead.

FUN FACT

The difference between a hoodoo and a pinnacle, or spire, is that hoodoos have a variable thickness and a shape similar to a totem pole. A spire, on the other hand, has a smoother profile and a more uniform thickness that tapers from the ground upward.

SIDE TRIP

Arches National Park is home to more than 2,000 named arches, as well as other natural sculptures—domes, walls, spires and even formations resembling giant chess pieces.
nps.gov/arch

▼
Visit the Toadstools for up-close views of unique rock formations.

Fold, a 100-mile-long wrinkle in the earth's crust.

The rock layers on the west side of the park have been lifted more than 7,000 feet higher than those on the east side. Wind and water have carved the tilted layers of sandstone into rainbow-tinted mesas, spires, monoliths, arches and massive domes (resembling the Capitol Building in Washington, D.C.). The roads here provide grand views of the rock formations, with an added dash of color in spring and summer, when wildflowers decorate the desert in vibrant hues.

Traveling between the parks, you can drive all 124 miles of the byway in three easy hours, and you'll enjoy every minute of the ride. The view from the main road is dominated by fire-red rock sprinkled with pinyon pine and juniper. It all lies in majestic loneliness under bright blue skies occasionally broken by unhurried clouds.

The smooth paved byway snakes up, over and through a topographically diverse landscape. Like the parks on either end of it, the road seems to offer glimpses of a fantastic new world every few miles. While those glimpses really are wonderful, the real payoff comes from taking the time to explore.

State parks, national recreation areas and monuments, alpine forests, historic pioneer towns and natural collections of stone carvings both immense and bizarre beckon from the side roads that Utah aptly refers to as scenic backways.

Among my favorites is Cottonwood Canyon Road, a backway that leads to the beautiful red-rock chimneys of Kodachrome Basin State Park and a giant double arch of blond sandstone called Grosvenor Arch.

Take Hole-in-the-Rock Road (which is mostly well-maintained gravel) about 40 miles to see Sunset Arch. Somewhat incongruously, I like to photograph it at sunrise, but it's impressive at any time of day. This scenic backway also provides access to a number of other recreational and historic sites in both Grand Staircase-Escalante National Monument and Glen Canyon National Recreation Area, including Devils Garden, Dry Fork Narrows and Dance Hall Rock.

A 3-mile trail just off the highway between Escalante and Boulder leads to Lower Calf Creek Falls, where a silky spray of water descends 126 feet over coral-tinted sandstone. The deep pool below is a popular swimming spot, so come prepared to take a dip!

Despite these occasional oases, the land in this part of Utah receives only 10 to 15 inches of rain a year, so the flora and fauna are highly adapted to desert conditions. I like to shoot the numerous cacti in close-up compositions. And if you're lucky enough to be here when the rains do come, the wildflower bloom that follows is breathtaking.

There's also a surprising variety of wildlife here. I often catch glimpses of coyotes, jackrabbits, roadrunners and pronghorns, but they usually stay beyond the range of even my longest telephoto lens.

I've been exploring the photographic possibilities of this area for years, and I've still barely scratched the surface. So, while you could drive Scenic Byway 12 in three easy hours, I suggest you slow down and take the time to truly enjoy one of the most beautiful and unique landscapes in America. You'll be glad you did. ❀

▼

Bryce Point offers iconic views of the sprawling Bryce Ampitheatre.

Waves crash upon the rocks beneath Lime Kiln Lighthouse, one of the best places in the world to see whales from land.

STORY BY
LESLIE FORSBERG

SAN JUAN ISLANDS

WRITER LESLIE FORSBERG BOARDS A FERRY AND SAVORS THE
GOOD LIFE ON WASHINGTON'S SAN JUAN ISLANDS.

STANDING AT THE windswept bow of the ferry as it motors west through the cobalt waters of the Salish Sea, we watch as forested islands, sepia toned in the late-afternoon sun, slide into view and then recede in our frothy wake. Behind us, glacier-clad Mount Baker is fixed to the eastern horizon. Floating through the archipelago on our most recent journey to the San Juan Islands, my partner, Brian, and I find ourselves becoming increasingly relaxed, lulled by the soothing vibration and the sense that we've gone beyond the boundaries of our busy daily lives into a tranquil and welcoming space.

Situated between Washington state and British Columbia, the 172 isles that make up the San Juan Islands offer a plethora of opportunities to soak in the beauty of nature, explore a vibrant arts scene, pursue outdoor adventures and indulge in a bounty of local foods, from oysters and wild-harvested fish to fresh fruits and vegetables.

These days the islands are especially alluring for their isolation. Only a few of the islands are accessible via public transport, so the number of visitors is naturally limited. The Washington State Ferries meander through the islands on a spectacularly scenic route, traveling from the city of Anacortes on the mainland to San Juan, Lopez and Orcas islands.

San Juan, the largest and most populated island, has fun diversions and some drop-dead gorgeous settings, including miles of beaches. The ferry docks at Friday Harbor, where shops, cafes and galleries jostle down to the water's edge.

The beauty of the islands inspires artists of all genres. At WaterWorks Gallery, we admire vivid contemporary paintings of the red-barked madrone trees that fringe the islands. And at Arctic Raven Gallery, masterful Native American carvings lend the place a reverential air. Nearby, the San Juan

Points of INTEREST

REST STOP

For more than 40 years, Holly B's Bakery on Lopez Island has been serving up tasty breads and pastries to local residents and visitors alike. Be sure to try one of the cinnamon rolls! *hollybsbakery.com*

NOT TO BE MISSED

San Juan Island is one of the best places on Earth for whale watching. May through September, orcas, gray whales, humpbacks and minke whales swim past Lime Kiln Point State Park on the west side of the island. Do a deep dive into whales at the Lime Kiln Point Interpretive Center. *parks.wa.gov*

NEARBY ATTRACTION

The Orcas Island Historical Museum is housed within six original homestead cabins from the late 1800s. Visit the complex to peruse thousands of local artifacts and photographs and learn what life was like for the early settlers and Native American communities in this area. *orcasmuseums.org*

▼

Boats float beneath a canopy of fog and sunlight in Friday Harbor.

Islands Museum of Art celebrates contemporary art from around the Northwest and beyond.

We could linger for hours in town, but there's so much more to see. We're bound for a familiar touchstone, Roche Harbor Resort, where the historic 1886 Hotel de Haro holds timeless appeal. A guest book in the lobby bears the faded signature of a special guest: President Theodore Roosevelt, who paid a visit here in 1903.

Fortified by gourmet sandwiches from the resort's Lime Kiln Cafe, we stroll along docks filled with gleaming yachts and imagine hitching a ride.

Near the resort's entrance, we marvel at works of art in the San Juan Islands

Sculpture Park before heading out in pursuit of more history.

In 1859 the Pig War, precipitated by a free-roaming pig rooting through an American's potato patch, set off military escalations between England and the United States, both of which claimed the island. War ships rallied and fortifications were built—English Camp on the north end and American Camp on the south.

The laid-back feel of the islands clearly worked its charm: Both forces ended up dancing and celebrating the holidays together before reaching an accord (and peace) 12 years later. Today both camps are open as part of the San Juan Island National Historical Park.

English Camp, on a placid bay, has an air of British formality to it, with a tidy blockhouse and a traditional English garden surrounded by a picket fence. In contrast, American Camp is a broad, open prairie sloping down to driftwood-tangled beaches. The exceptionally rare island marble butterfly is found only here. Brian and I search for pretty pebbles and skip rocks at 2-mile-long South Beach under the watchful gaze of deer grazing nearby.

At day's end, we toast to the islands at Duck Soup, one of the area's best restaurants. Just down the road, at Wescott Bay Shellfish, we savor plump, sweet oysters harvested that morning. The night is spent minutes away in a Lakedale Resort yurt with modern Scandinavian decor.

Driving off the dock the next morning on Lopez Island, we're greeted by locals heading to the ferry, who nod and wave as we pass. "Slowpez," as it's known locally, is also called "the friendly isle."

Lopez is compact and has gentle terrain, making it perfect for cycling. Farm fields are dotted with sheep and bisected by idyllic country lanes, with several standout beaches for picnicking and relaxing. Renting bicycles in the island's commercial hub, Lopez Village, Brian and I stop by the legendary Holly B's Bakery for the cinnamon rolls that I always crave once I've returned home.

Spencer Spit—a 200-acre state park known for hiking, wildlife-watching and clamming—is a longtime favorite of mine. Brian and I stroll a sand spit and then watch a great blue heron stalking minnows in a lagoon where birdsong echoes.

Later, we cycle around the curved arm of Fisherman's Bay and through a fragrant cedar forest to a heritage orchard and beach, part of a land trust. A bit farther south, at Shark Reef Sanctuary, a park reached by a short trail, we watch as harbor seals roll and play, glistening in the sun.

From June to September, lavender blooms in local farm fields.

San Juan County Park has gorgeous views of Haro Strait.

In contrast to level Lopez, horseshoe-shaped Orcas is heavily wooded and hilly. The bustling village of Eastsound, situated at the center of the horseshoe, has a vacation vibe, with galleries and boutiques filled with art, souvenirs and fashionable clothing.

The island's charms have drawn the attention of Oprah Winfrey; in 2018 she bought several downtown buildings and a gated estate with a half-mile of waterfront. Darvill's Bookstore, which is located in one of Oprah's buildings on Main Street, sells books for readers of all sorts and boasts an enviable view of the bay and islands.

We're thrilled to find that same view when we check into our lodging for the night, the new Water's Edge Suite at the Outlook Inn in the heart of town. Lounging in our well-appointed room will have to wait for the evening—we're ready to explore.

At Cascade Falls, in Moran State Park, a trail through mossy woods leads to a series of cascades rimmed by massive old-growth trees. I wrap my arms around one, and they reach less than a third of the way. Farther south, at Obstruction Pass State Park, we hike through woods filled with sword ferns and glossy-leafed salal to a nice perch atop a boulder on the beach.

As the sun begins to set, we drive to the top of Mount Constitution, Orcas Island's 2,409-foot peak, and climb to the top of a stone observation tower for a truly breathtaking view of the water and islands. On the southern horizon, nearly 200 miles away, Mount Rainier gleams in the sun. On the northern horizon, we can make out a few of the buildings in Vancouver—from here, they resemble tiny, beige Legos. Bald eagles soar on thermals below us, and cliff swallows whirl in a space so vast they resemble a cloud of butterflies.

The breeze stills, and I pause to take in the beauty of this place, a tranquil oasis in an incomparable archipelago in the upper left-hand corner of the contiguous U.S. ◗

Wyoming

STORY BY
JEFF TESTER

YELLOWSTONE

AFTER HIS WIFE, LESA, BEAT BREAST CANCER, JEFF TESTER
EMBRACED LIFE—AND AMERICA'S NATIONAL PARKS.

OUR STORY STARTED with a wake-up call on Feb. 2, 2001. Only our wake-up call did not come from the front desk of a hotel. Our call was from the office of my wife's physician.

At 37 years old, Lesa was diagnosed with breast cancer. For the next year, this brave lady endured surgeries, chemo and radiation treatments and the loss of her hair. That was the year I found out how strong and how tough breast cancer patients have to be to battle this awful disease.

When Lesa was free of cancer, we dedicated the following year to healing. During that time, Lesa and I discussed the future. We had been salting away almost every penny we could to retire early and travel, but this wake-up call made us want to travel now.

Having been raised in the shadow of Great Smoky Mountains National Park in Tennessee, Lesa and I were instinctively drawn to America's scenic showpieces. In the 20 years since Lesa's recovery, we have visited 26 national parks, from Acadia in Maine to Denali in Alaska. Yellowstone in Wyoming remains one of our favorites.

DANIEL VIÑÉ GARCIA/GETTY IMAGES

▼

Vibrant Grand Prismatic Spring is the largest hot spring in the park.

Points of INTEREST

REST STOP

The historic Old Faithful Inn offers views of the world-famous geyser along with homey comforts. The inn, which was built more than a century ago, is also the largest log cabin in the world, and bookings there are highly sought after. *nps.gov/places/000/old-faithful-inn*

NOT TO BE MISSED

A visit to Mammoth Hot Springs will reveal some of Yellowstone's most hauntingly beautiful thermal theatrics. The springs take their delicate colors from the algae and bacteria that thrive in the steamy water. Among the most active of the terraces are Opal Terrace and Minerva Terrace.

FUN FACT

Of the 500 or so active geysers in the world, more than 200 are found in Yellowstone.

WORDS TO THE WISE

Most park roads are closed from November through April, but park snowmobiles can be rented in winter.

▼

Jeff and Lesa enjoy the beautiful view from atop Pothole Dome.

Yellowstone was the United States' first designated national park, so we thought, Why not start with the first? After booking the flight, a rental car and lodging and then seeing the cost, I was about to reconsider our new life plan. But Lesa reminded me to live in the present, and away we went.

We flew into Jackson Hole, Wyoming. As our plane circled the airport on a cloudless, sunny day, our eyes became fixed on the mountains. It was fall, so the leaves of aspen trees draped along the mountain slopes looked like a fine scarf. And the valleys were covered with a colorful blanket woven from wildflowers and grasses. Lesa and I were in awe, and we had just left the airport. For the next nine days, each bend of the road seemed to reveal a landscape even more breathtaking than the last.

Whatever doubts we had about our new life plan melted away like butter on a hot biscuit. Lesa and I tried to imagine what the first mountain men thought as they walked through this magical place of geysers, hot springs

and wildlife. We were amazed by all that we saw, even though we had been carefully researching this park and planning for months.

We saw lumbering grizzly and black bears as they packed on the pounds in preparation for winter. One grizzly walked so close to the car that if it had turned its head to look in, it would have steamed up the window with its breath.

Wildlife was everywhere—packs of wolves in the Lamar Valley, grazing elk from the Grand Tetons to Mammoth Hot Springs, eagles soaring above the rivers and lakes as they hunted for unsuspecting fish, and, of course, thousands of roaming bison.

The trip etched memories that will stay with us forever. Lesa and I loved watching Old Faithful, the park's predictable geyser, erupt regularly throughout the day. The memory we cherish most, however, is the night when we cuddled up on a bench seat and watched the spectacular geyser beneath the white glow of a full moon. We sat there for a long time, soaking up the moment. ❧

JEFF TESTER

▼

Yellowstone is home to an estimated population of more than 700 grizzly bears.

Alaska's scenic Seward Highway offers twilight views of Turnagain Arm.

" Nature is not a place to visit. It is home."

—GARY SNYDER

SOUTHWEST

▼

Catalina Highway cuts through the desert landscape on its way to the summit of Mount Lemmon.

STORY BY
ROGER NAYLOR

CATALINA HIGHWAY

GO FROM THE DESERT TO ALPINE VISTAS ON THE SAME DAY ALONG THIS DRAMATIC DRIVE INTO THE CLOUDS.

FANTASTIC ROAD TRIPS aren't determined by the number of miles you drive but by the quality of those miles. By that standard, the winding road starting amid the suburbs of Tucson, Arizona, and snaking its way to the top of Mount Lemmon is an epic journey.

Catalina Highway, also known as Sky Island Scenic Byway, traverses only 27 miles, yet it is the biological equivalent of driving from Mexico to Canada. Travelers pass through five life zones as the paved road ascends from spiny desert scrub to mixed conifer forest. Every 1,000 feet gained in elevation is like traveling 600 miles to the north.

Starting out on Tanque Verde Road in northeast Tucson, turn north on Catalina Highway. For the first few miles, the road flashes across gently sloping hills and past suburban homes and bristling groves of saguaros, the tall stately cacti that define Arizona. The vast Sonoran Desert is the most biologically diverse one of all. This untended garden teems with plants and wildlife. The saguaros rise like lean

giants, quiet guardians at the base of Mount Lemmon.

Your destination is the highest point in the Santa Catalina Mountains, the rugged range that forms the northern border of Tucson. Mount Lemmon soars to 9,157 feet above sea level, so be prepared for temperatures to drop by 30 degrees or more on the drive. In Tucson, they like to boast that you can swim and ski in the same day, and this road proves it.

There's no need to rush to the top— there are plenty of convenient places to pull over along the paved two-lane highway, which twists, turns and switchbacks up the mountain. Here are a few not to be missed.

The tall saguaros marching up the slopes begin to disperse by the time the road cuts into steep-sided Molino Canyon. The overlook, which is about 5 miles up the Catalina Highway, offers a beautiful view down the boulder-strewn gorge. Two short trails branch off from the vista: One is wheelchair accessible, and the other is a bit more rugged but leads to a seasonal stream

Points of INTEREST

REST STOP
At the end of the drive, indulge in a cookie (try chocolate chip; oatmeal raisin; or the Rachel, with oats, butterscotch and coconut) at the Cookie Cabin in Summerhaven. *thecookiecabin.org*

NOT TO BE MISSED
The Mount Lemmon SkyCenter will dazzle stargazers with views of distant galaxies. The premier five-hour program starts two hours before sunset and includes a lecture, dinner and guided navigation of the night sky. Reservations are required. *skycenter .arizona.edu*

WORDS TO THE WISE
The byway is open year-round but winter weather and fire hazards may cause restrictions, so call ahead for conditions. Large motor homes over 22 feet may have trouble negotiating the steep grades and sharp turns. For more information, contact the Santa Catalina Ranger District at 520-749-8700 or visit *fs.usda.gov /coronado.*

▼

Many javelina—which are peccaries, not pigs!—call this area home.

that splashes over granite outcroppings shaded by willow, cottonwood and sycamore trees.

Past the viewpoint, the road crosses Molino Basin. Here, at an elevation of 4,500 feet, grasslands are dotted with oaks. Continuing about a mile farther, you will pass Gordon Hirabayashi Campground. Named for a Japanese-American student who challenged the legality of Japanese-American internment after the bombing of Pearl Harbor in 1941, the site was first established as a federal prison camp. Hirabayashi was sent there when he refused to report to an internment camp. The site was renamed to honor Hirabayashi in 1999, 12 years after the U.S. Supreme Court overturned his conviction. It's now a popular stop for hikers and bikers setting out on the Molino Basin Trail, a good connector route. Don't be surprised if you pass a few adventurous climbers making their way to angled cliffs lining a mighty and deep-cut gorge.

By the time you reach Windy Point, 14 miles from the desert floor, you're about halfway through the drive. This is the highway's preeminent overlook, set amid a terrace of jumbled stone and punctuated by rising pinnacles that attract seasoned rock climbers. Gazing out from the 6,400-foot perch, you'll have a spectacular view. The whole Tucson Basin spreads out below, and rows of mountains interrupt the city sprawl to define distant horizons. Such panoramas have turned Windy Point into something of an open-air cathedral—it's a a popular spot to hold weddings. So among the rock jocks, newlyweds, gawkers, picnickers and stargazers, Windy Point really does seem to offer something for everyone. A pedestrian crossing, a large parking area and restrooms help accommodate the steady stream of visitors.

If you haven't been impressed yet by the enormous engineering effort required to build this spectacular road, then you haven't been paying attention.

Frank Harris Hitchcock, a former editor of a local newspaper, spearheaded the movement to build the road. The construction began in 1933 and took nearly 18 years to complete.

The Palisades Visitor Center, located near the 20-mile mark, is a perfect place to pick up maps and hiking information or to learn about local wildlife. If you want to stretch your legs, the Butterfly Trail, supporting so much biologic diversity that it has been designated a Research Natural Area, slices through the forest just across the road.

The sky islands of southeastern Arizona are isolated mountain ranges rising dramatically from desert basins. These vertical refuges form islands of habitats—lush green forests high above the desert sea. Arizona may be known as a desert state, but don't overlook the soothing tree-clad oases floating above the heat and cacti.

As the road continues to switchback upward, you'll pass through forests of ponderosa pine. Pretty soon groves of pale-barked aspens appear, along with white and Douglas firs.

At mile 23, Aspen Vista offers the first amazing look to the north across the San Pedro Valley. You are above 8,000 feet now, and the saguaros and other cacti are long since forgotten.

Nearing mile 25, you'll approach a highway junction. Turn right to head toward Ski Valley or continue straight another quarter-mile for a welcome taste of civilization at Summerhaven, a small hamlet along wooded Sabino Creek. Here you'll find a general store and a couple of restaurants, including the Cookie Cabin (which is known for its Frisbee-sized cookies).

Most of Summerhaven tragically burned down in a 2003 fire, but cabins and businesses were rebuilt and the community persevered. No one wanted to let go of this little piece of paradise.

The road continues past the village for another scenic mile, ending at the

As you drive, desert basins morph into lush forest scenes.

▼

The granite spires attract climbers, who upon reaching the top are treated to amazing views of surrounding mountains.

Saguaro cacti are familiar figures along the highway.

Marshall Gulch Picnic Area along Sabino Creek. This also serves as a trailhead for popular hikes, including the 4-mile Aspen Loop, which combines part of the Marshall Gulch Trail and the Aspen Trail. It's a lovely shady hike with long-ranging views when the forest canopy breaks apart. During busy times, parking can be scarce.

Returning to the junction and then turning left will lead you to Ski Valley, the southernmost ski area in the United States. A total of 21 runs carve up these slopes in winter. In warmer months, the chairlift operates as a scenic ride. It's a wonderful way to see the fall foliage that graces the forests.

The last stretch of highway, now a twisting gravel road, makes its way to the summit trailheads. Try the Meadow and Mount Lemmon Trail #5 Loop for a gentle 2.1-mile stroll.

At the top of Mount Lemmon is a working observatory, open to the public only during specific events. The Mount Lemmon SkyCenter has two of the largest telescopes in the Southwest trained on the night sky.

As you finally turn back from its peak, you may wonder how this stately mountain got its name. It's named for Sara Plummer Lemmon, an artist and botanist who became the first white woman to scale the peak. She made the climb with her new husband, another botanist, in 1881. They spent their honeymoon collecting a wide range of plants and specimens, some of which were previously undiscovered. And they did it along the length of a single mountain, not spread across the land from Mexico to Canada.

The journey is as remarkable today as it was back then. ◾

STORY BY
ELLIE PIPER

MESILLA

THIS TOWN SPARKLES WITH CHRISTMAS LIGHTS.

LUMINARIAS ARE A holiday mainstay throughout the state of New Mexico. Albuquerque's lights span entire neighborhoods and Santa Fe boasts glorious luminaria processions, but there's something especially stirring about the Christmas Eve display in Mesilla, a small town just east of the Rio Grande.

Mesilla's backstory is peppered with Wild West lore. Infamous outlaw Billy the Kid was sentenced to hang here in 1881. (He escaped.) And the influence of Native, Spanish, Mexican and other communities creates a vibrant cultural tapestry, evident in the town's adobe architecture, galleries, eateries and churches—notably the Basilica of San Albino on the historic plaza.

The town's luminaria tradition began back in the mid-1960s, when Josefina Gamboa Biel Emerson moved into her parents' home near the basilica. In keeping with family practice, she set out luminarias, inviting guests in for food and drink. In time, her display grew larger and more elaborate. Local Boy Scouts helped place the lights; merchants gave to the candle fund.

Today, the Las Cruces High School marching band and Los Leones de Mesilla (the local Lions Club) help sustain the custom, filling paper bags with sand and votives. Locals distribute them throughout the plaza and along the Avenida de Mesilla, and the candles are lit in unison. Come sunset, the plaza is bustling with revelers and carolers and 6,000 flickering lights.

For a memorable daytime excursion, head 2 miles southwest to Bosque State Park, an Audubon-designated birding area with inviting trails and views of the Organ Mountains to the east. In town, check out the historic Fountain Theatre, the Mesilla Book Center, and green-chile-smothered everything at Andele Restaurante. And if you're here at Christmastime, by all means, take in the spectacular lights. ▪

Top:◄
Luminarias
and string
lights brighten
Mesilla on
Christmas Eve.
Bottom:
Watchful
birders may
spot sandhill
cranes at
the Mesilla
Valley Bosque
State Park.

Points of INTEREST

REST STOP

Popular restaurant La Posta de Mesilla has been serving up delicious Mexican food and steaks since 1939. The building it's housed in has an even longer history: Beginning in 1857, it was used as a stop for Butterfield Overland Mail stagecoaches on their route between St. Louis and San Francisco. *lapostademesilla .com*

WORDS TO THE WISE

While the Christmas lights make winters here spectacular, there's plenty to see and do in Mesilla all year long. Check out the Mesilla Events calendar before you plan your trip. *mesillanm.gov*

SIDE TRIP

Most national and state parks forbid the removal of any natural objects, but Rockhound State Park encourages prospecting. The parkland is rich in semiprecious stones, including jasper, opal, and blue agate. Enjoy a day hike in the area or make an overnight stop (the park is close to Interstate 10).

STORY AND PHOTOS BY
PAULINE RINGER

ELK CITY

EXPERIENCE SMALL-TOWN CHARM AND UNIQUE ATTRACTIONS ALONG THIS STRETCH OF OLD ROUTE 66.

ROLLING THROUGH THE plains of western Oklahoma can seem a bit desolate for some tourists, but small-town country life still flourishes on the Mother Road, old Route 66.

Elk City has always stood out to me among these towns. Maybe it's the warmth of the people, the peace and quiet, the charming vintage homes that grace the brick streets in the historical district, the open plains that melt into an endless sky or the windmills that grace the horizon.

The town is also home to one of my favorite attractions, the National Route 66 Museum, which is located at the west end of town on old Route 66. About 400 miles of the 2,448-mile route wind through Oklahoma. The museum is full of memorabilia from the Mother Road, including vintage cars, and it tells the story of the people who lived or traveled here.

It's not unusual to see motorcycle groups or tour buses rolling down Route 66, which becomes Third Street in Elk City. While taking photographs at the museum last year, I met a group of bikers from Finland who were trekking the full length of the Mother Road from Chicago to Los Angeles. Bikers are a special breed: It takes serious dedication and perseverance to travel 2,448 miles on two wheels, enduring the changing weather (and bugs in your teeth). The love of the ride requires a tough hide!

The National Route 66 Museum is part of the larger Elk City Museum Complex, which is a must-see in town (Paul McCartney reportedly stopped by while cruising Route 66 for his 66th birthday). The other museums at the complex are the Old Town Museum (learn how Oklahoma's early pioneers once lived), the Blacksmith Museum

Points of INTEREST

REST STOP

At Major Bean Coffee & Sandwich Co., road-weary visitors can choose from several varieties of fresh-brewed coffee, as well as pastries, soups and salads. The cafe is housed in a historic building, and the owners have stayed true to its original spirit. *major -bean-coffee.com*

SIDE TRIP

The Metcalfe Museum in Durham offers a glimpse into the hardship and the rugged beauty of ranch life in the 19th century. Local pioneer woman Augusta Corson Metcalfe painted detailed depictions that eventually gained her renown as the Sagebrush Artist; many of her works are on display here, along with artifacts and re-creations of historical buildings. *metcalfemuseum.org*

NEARBY ATTRACTION

220-acre Ackley Park boasts a carousel and train ride for kids, a mile-long walking trail through oaks and cedars and a lighthouse that adds a touch of whimsy to the area.

Visitors come from all over the world (including Finland!) to ride along old Route 66.

▼

Vintage farm equipment and memorabilia are on display at the Elk City Museum Complex.

(see how steel was once forged), the Farm and Ranch Museum (take a peek at old-fashioned farm tools) and the National Transportation Museum (sit for a few minutes in the drive-in theater and watch snippets of classic movies).

You're in for a treat if you visit the Blacksmith Museum when curator Bob Kennemer is at work. Curious visitors can watch Bob craft gates, railings, horseshoes, utensils and weapons.

The Farm and Ranch Museum, known by everyone here as "the big red barn," is another favorite of mine. Inside the barn you'll find vintage cars, windmills, tractors, a kitchen from the 1800s and a cotton gin. It's fun to look around the barn and imagine yourself walking back in time.

The complex's courtyard features a replica of a small town circa the late 1800s that reminds me of *Little House on the Prairie*. As I stroll around the tidy courtyard, I can almost envision a tall gent from long ago, tipping his hat to a lady passing by the mercantile in a long skirt and petticoat.

Whether you are looking for an adventure on Route 66 or just breezing through on the tail of an Oklahoma wind, Elk City is a sweet refuge from the road. ✒

Texas

STORY BY
EMMA RHYNE

PINEY WOODS

EXPERIENCE THE MAJESTIC BEAUTY AND ENDURING CHARM OF THIS SYLVAN TEXAS GEM.

ALL AROUND OUR little house in the woods, an East Texas autumn engulfs us with life and the vibrant colors of auburn maple trees; rich brown oak leaves; and resilient, green, ever-present pines. From the rolling pastures where the longhorns graze, the chilling wind brushes past our cheeks.

When fall settles in this special part of the world, there's nowhere more beautiful than the Piney Woods.

Covering 23,000 square miles, this patch of northeast Texas is home to an abundance of natural beauty nestled between the pines' whispering green needles. Summer is hot; winter is a week long, if we're lucky; and autumn is just about perfect.

The Piney Woods is a must-see for your next fall vacation. The natural beauty of our soft hills, blanketed by thick forests of evergreen and oak, surpasses expectations. In little towns

▼

Mast Arboretum features myriad themed gardens and is free to visit.

ROBERTA SMITH

REST STOPS

Stay in Nacogdoches long enough and you're bound to see someone you know at Dolli's Diner. From old-fashioned pancakes to honest burgers and fries, this family-oriented restaurant has that old-town feel with friendly service. *facebook.com /Dollis-Diner*

At the General Mercantile and Oldtime String Shop in downtown Nacogdoches, take a trip back in time as you browse shelves full of antique toys and handcarved musical instruments. *visitnacogdoches.org*

NOT TO BE MISSED

There is nothing quite like the Fortney Home. Sit in the lap of a giant gorilla statue or marvel at tiny figurines from foreign lands lying next to BlackBerry phones. This unusual shop is a collector's dream—and will be fun for anyone who's looking for a coat rack shaped like a shoe. *fortneyhome .com*

▼

Fishing and bird-watching are favorite pastimes in the Piney Woods.

tucked under the changing trees, there are secrets, stories and hidden adventures waiting to charm, amaze and inspire whoever happens to stumble upon them.

I grew up in Tyler, the largest town in the region, which means roses have bloomed in my life for as long as I can remember. Pink petals and bristling thorns surrounded my house and most buildings in the area.

Tyler's nickname, the rose capital of America, comes from its booming rose industry, which today exports $50 million worth of blooms a year. America's largest rose garden, the 14-acre Tyler Municipal Rose Garden, provides visitors with an ideal place for a picnic. Rows of beautiful rosebushes bloom in October and May, and ponds, fountains and archways give structure to the blooms.

The sweet scent of the flowers floats leisurely through the Texas humidity, enchanting visitors and locals alike. Inside the visitors center, you'll find a museum displaying dresses, historical

facts and memorabilia from the Texas Rose Festival, a pageant showcasing the Texas Rose Parade. During the parade, the Texas Rose Queen and her court greet the waiting onlookers with stately waves and fantastic dresses. If you plan a visit to Tyler, be sure to catch the annual festival to see a celebration of elegance in the streets.

Although Tyler roses are stunning, the Piney Woods isn't all delicate petals and pageant shows. The people who live in the depths of East Texas enjoy a life spent outdoors, connected to the nature that surrounds the area—both domesticated and a bit less predictable. Along with many other exceptional parks and gardens, Lake Palestine, a reservoir in the Tyler area, engages the wilder side of visitors and native Tylerites alike.

If catching a record bass is your idea of a perfect vacation, look no further than Lake Fork. This slice of watery paradise is a fishing dream come true. Lake Fork holds the record for 34 of the 50 largest bass caught in the state. The saying is true: Everything's bigger in Texas! Another area with excellent fishing and even better camping is Lake o' the Pines. Surrounded by parks and campgrounds, this reservoir in Marion County is known as the best in Texas for canoeing, camping and taking in the beauty of the Piney Woods. Adorning its shoreline and the many islets are herons, scissor-tailed flycatchers and occasional bald eagles. Bring the RV or a tent and bask in the balmy weather and bird-watching on a fall weekend by the lake.

Caddo Lake State Park also belongs on your must-see list. Caddo Lake lies under a gentle spread of cypress trees. Dangling tendrils of Spanish moss and a constant mist create a feeling of mystical awe as visitors fish, canoe or kayak or simply enjoy the sights around the giant reservoir.

The park is teeming with wildlife, boasting more than 70 species of fish. Alligators and snakes also call this area home, so be sure to keep a lookout. If you choose to spend the night, you can find many camping sites, historic cabins and RV parks nearby. You'll relish the extra hours—visiting Caddo Lake immerses you in a pocket of the world filled with dreamy beauty and endless possibilities.

Campers and hikers will find their Piney Woods paradise in Daingerfield State Park. From simply roughing it in sleeping bags to reserving historic cabins with showers and kitchens, plenty of great options are available for visitors interested in hiking the multitude of trails throughout the park. If you want to stick around for a spell after your camping adventure, the popcorn at the Daingerfield movie theater is reputed to be the best in all of Texas.

Whether you're looking to fish, bird-watch or just have a fun day at the lake, East Texas' mild winters and beautiful lakes provide a place for you

The Victorian Fortney Home looks traditional but sells eclectic wares.

▼
Cypress trees stand tall in Caddo Lake State Park, where several waterways create a playground for canoers.

Tyler's 14-acre Municipal Rose Garden is home to more than 500 varieties of roses.

to experience a wild and untamed natural heritage guarded under evergreen pines.

In this natural setting, the towns of the Piney Woods fascinate visitors with their diverse cultures. From Jacksonville (known in the 1930s as the tomato capital of the world) to Canton (home of the First Monday Trade Days flea market), they have a lot to offer. The small city of Nacogdoches might be the most interesting of all. When visiting, be sure to stop in the antique stores or one of the many coffee shops, such as Nine Flags Coffee Roasters, and ask a BIN (a local who was "born in Nac") about some of the hidden treasures that tourists might miss.

For example, BINs know to visit the Mast Arboretum, a garden designed by college students, in the mornings, when the mists linger between sculptures created by generations of artists. They know that of the many parks in Nac, Pecan Acres Park provides a special trail along the edge of burbling Lanana Creek. And they know to visit Fortney Home, an antique shop to end all antique shops. All these places and more showcase the unique culture of the oldest town in Texas.

These are only a few of the towns that give the Piney Woods its incredible charm, which you can experience for yourself if you happen to wander our way when the leaves start to change. You won't be disappointed if you do. All my life I've found sanctuary, adventure and history underneath these whispering pines, where nature enchants like nowhere else.

Here, rolling hills along the riversides and lakefronts burn bright with the colors of fall.

Roses are blooming again.

The Piney Woods await. ●

Follow a red brick road to the heart of Nacogdoches, the oldest town in Texas.

"For my part, I travel not to go anywhere, but to go. I travel for travel's sake."

—ROBERT LOUIS STEVENSON

Brilliant fall foliage adorns the Garden of the Gods Recreation Area in the Shawnee National Forest.

STORY BY
LORI VANOVER

SHAWNEE NATIONAL FOREST

THE LUSH FORESTS OF SOUTHERN ILLINOIS SHELTER NATURAL WONDERS THAT WILL RECHARGE YOUR SPIRIT.

THE FIRST TIME I visited southern Illinois with my husband, Dirk, I was mostly looking forward to the award-winning barbecue, fresh peach cobbler and local wines. I was raised in north-central Illinois, where the landscape is mostly prairies and cornfields, and I have to admit I had no idea there were any natural wonders hidden away in the 286,000-acre Shawnee National Forest.

The food and wine were well worth the drive. I also got the chance to meet Dirk's relatives who live in Cobden, a friendly village known for its unusual school mascot, the Appleknockers. We now try to visit at least once a year.

Usually we just spend a few relaxing days in the countryside, sipping and socializing along the Shawnee Hills Wine Trail. But a couple of years ago, we took a wrong turn on one of the winding, densely forested roads and arrived in the Crab Orchard National Wildlife Refuge.

As I wondered about what creatures found sanctuary in the surrounding woods, I realized that southern Illinois is our sanctuary too. My curiosity was piqued to explore more of the wild and wonderful Shawnee Hills region.

We started this year's trip to the area at the Little Grand Canyon, a deep box canyon carved by water erosion near Pomona. Two hiking trails combine to form a 3-mile loop. We opted to descend to the canyon; the other direction offers views of the Big Muddy River and the Mississippi River floodplain.

After hiking about a mile, we reached a canyon overlook that peers down over a mature oak and hickory forest. Here the pathway cuts sharply to the left and disappears into a streambed.

We walked carefully alongside steep bluffs over wet sandstone rocks and mud. If you hike here, be sure to follow the white diamond trail markers and watch for handholds and steps carved

Points of INTEREST

REST STOPS

Stop in Marion or Murphysboro for a meal at 17th Street Barbecue. Pitmaster Mike Mills has won multiple awards for his pulled pork, ribs and beef brisket. *17thstreetbarbecue.com*

Giant City Lodge is famous for its hearty all-you-can-eat fried chicken dinners served with all the fixings. *giantcitylodge.com*

FUN FACT

Shawnee National Forest is home to Sand Cave, which is the largest known sandstone cave in North America.

NEARBY ATTRACTION

The Crab Orchard National Wildlife Refuge is a popular stopping place for migratory waterfowl on the Mississippi Flyway. Vast flights of Canada geese and ducks, as well as common loons and green herons, can usually be found here. Visitors to the refuge can make use of various hiking trails, observation towers, docks and swimming beaches. *fws.gov/refuge /crab-orchard*

▼

The rock formations at Garden of the Gods offer stunning views.

by the Civilian Conservation Corps in the 1930s. The glorious silence of the forest was punctuated only by chirping songbirds and buzzing cicadas.

If you're looking for an easier hike, check out the Pomona Natural Bridge. Also nearby is Highway 2, also known as Skyline Drive, which offers gorgeous overlooks of Bald Knob—the highest peak in southern Illinois. A number of cabins and bed-and-breakfasts line this scenic road.

After a good night's rest, we headed to the Henry Barkhausen Wetlands Center at the Cache River State Natural Area, known for centuries-old cypress and tupelo trees. It's also the starting point of Tunnel Hill State Trail. This bike path built over former railroad tracks stretches more than 45 miles north to

Harrisburg—the home of the Shawnee National Forest headquarters. Several miles of Tunnel Hill State Trail follow the Trail of Tears, the path taken by the Cherokee Nation during its forced relocation to Oklahoma in 1838 and 1839, and the River to River Trail, which runs from the Mississippi to the Ohio.

We had the trail all to ourselves other than a few bird-watchers. Local wildlife was plentiful: We spotted warblers and swallows, as well as needlenose garfish, painted turtles and a mink.

Back at the wetlands center, a helpful guide gave us directions to see the giant cypress trees. After a quick drive, we arrived a small parking area named Big Cypress Access. Within just a few steps, the massive, ancient specimens came into view.

These are no ordinary trees—they are 1,000 years old and more than 40 feet in circumference. It's astounding to think about how the world has changed while they've grown.

Northeast of here you'll find myriad geological wonders at Garden of the Gods. Magnificent, otherworldly stone formations tower over 3,300 acres of forested wilderness. It's hard for me to believe that this is in the same state where I grew up.

We chose to hike the Observation Trail, which takes you close to giant marvels such as Camel Rock and Monkey Face. Adventurous visitors can climb up onto the rocks for jaw-dropping views and watch as raptors soar through the sky at eye level. This place definitely encourages you to bask in the glory of nature and soak up the region's beauty. But remember to be careful and use common sense—it is a very steep drop off the rocks.

We spent our final day at Giant City State Park in Makanda. Dirk has fond memories of family reunions here, and during our visit the park was bustling with activity.

If you wish to extend your stay in the park, there are several campgrounds to choose from. You'll also find charming cabins near the Giant City Lodge, built by the CCC in 1939.

We followed directions to the Giant City Nature Trail, which features the famous "streets" of Giant City. These magnificent rock walls look like the sides of buildings, creating the illusion of an urban cityscape in the middle of the woods. We also hiked to see Devil's Standtable, a towering sandstone pillar, and looked for native wildflowers on the Trillium Trail.

As our time in southern Illinois came to an end, we felt rejuvenated. We're already planning what to see on next year's trip. I don't think I'll ever get tired of exploring the wonders of this restorative refuge. ❀

Giant cypress trees preside over the Cache River State Natural Area.

STORY BY
DAVE HARRIS

NASHVILLE

THIS HIDDEN GEM KEEPS ONE COUPLE COMING BACK.

MY WIFE, KACY, AND I first visited Brown County, Indiana, on our honeymoon in 1998. Eighteen years and nine children later, Brown County has become an annual romantic getaway for us, and sometimes the whole family tags along.

Nashville is a hidden gem tucked away in the hills and trees. There are special stores, great places to stay and excellent restaurants along Van Buren Street and the connecting roads.

As I said, we have nine kids. So when we have a chance for a break, Kacy and I like to go somewhere where we can relax and unwind. Here, the days just seem to have a smooth flow to them.

We like to stay at Cornerstone Inn or Artists Colony Inn and sleep with the windows open. That way, we wake up to the sound of happy people checking out the nearby stores and restaurants.

In Nashville, most of the shops close down at 5, so that's when we choose to arrive. We use this time to play a card game, enjoy some quiet conversation or ride in a horse-drawn carriage.

One of my favorite things to do that first night is to take a midnight stroll. Everything is within walking distance, so Kacy and I just talk, look around and enjoy one another's company. As we do some window-shopping, we think about where we will go the next day.

When the morning arrives, we enjoy breakfast at our inn and then hit the town. The streets are always bustling in the daytime. We visit certain places every year, but we always tend to find something new.

The Brown County Art Gallery, one of the oldest in the country, opened in Nashville in 1926, and the region is known as an art colony. Many local artists' works can be found for sale at the shops.

When the kids come with us, we often go to the Abe Martin Lodge in Brown County State Park. There, you can rent a room at the main building or a cabin in the woods. The kids have lots of fun playing on the cabin's back porch and at the indoor water park. There's also a restaurant and some quiet picnic spots.

We have made several trips to Brown County over the years, and we never tire of it. The kids always say this is the "best vacation ever" and look forward to going back. ◖

Points of INTEREST

REST STOP

To start your day off with a boost, head to the Daily Grind Coffee House & Cafe for a warm drink and a quick bite. *nashvilledailygrind .com*

Stop by The Nashville House on South Van Buren Street to taste the famous fried biscuits and other homey fare. *nashvillehousebc .com*

NOT TO BE MISSED

The Bill Monroe Memorial Bean Blossom Bluegrass Festival is held annually in June. It's the oldest festival in the world dedicated to Monroe's "high lonesome" bluegrass songs. *billmonroemusicpark .com*

NEARBY ATTRACTION

Brown County State Park is a few miles east of town. Once across the small covered bridge at its entrance, visitors can explore nearly 16,000 acres of woodland, lakes and streams. Hike a shady trail, ride a horse or watch for waterfowl. *on.in.gov/brown countysp*

THE BROWN COUNTY CONVENTION AND VISITORS BUREAU

▼

The lawn of the historic Brown County Courthouse is a popular gathering place in Nashville.

▼
A gorgeous sunset paints the sky over an old corncrib in Dallas County, Iowa.

STORY AND PHOTOS BY
JUSTIN ROGERS

NORTHEAST REGION

UNCOVER IOWA'S TREASURES, FROM SCENIC RIVER BLUFFS TO ROLLING FARMLAND—AND GENUINE KINDNESS.

MANY PEOPLE THINK Iowa is just another flyover state. But anyone familiar with the region can tell you Iowa is so much more than that. So what draws folks to the heart of the Midwest? Maybe it's the affordable living. Or the stunning sunrises and sunsets over gentle rolling hills. Or the mantra of "Iowa Nice" that greets those passing through.

Spreading kindness is a core value in Iowa. Take, for example, the "Iowa wave" at Iowa Hawkeyes university football games in Iowa City. After the first quarter, everyone in the stadium turns and waves across the street to the University of Iowa Children's Hospital. Inside, patients and their families wave back. Even the opposing team waves.

Beyond kindness, Iowa holds other treasures. My wife, Jonah, and I live in Des Moines, but we are both from Fort Dodge, in the north-central part of the state. We enjoy the beauty of the four seasons, and we appreciate living close to family.

From our perspective, Iowa is flat and sprawling. But once you head northeast from Des Moines, it's amazing just how many hills there are.

Iowa's entire eastern border is carved out by the Mississippi River, the second-longest river in North America. Last fall I took a three-day photography trip to that gorgeous region, focusing my efforts on the state's northeast corner.

I started my journey in Winneshiek County, home of the small college town of Decorah. Here, Palisades Park sits on a bluff east of the Upper Iowa River and provides an excellent vantage point from which to view Decorah. Another must-see spot is Dunnings Spring Park, which is home to a 200-foot waterfall—Iowa's tallest.

From Decorah, I followed River Road along the Upper Iowa River and then hopped to the east to connect with the Driftless Area Scenic Byway, a 100-mile stretch that zigzags across beautiful Allamakee County. Heading northeast,

Points of INTEREST

NOT TO BE MISSED

Among the 200-plus prehistoric mounds at Effigy Mounds National Monument, the Great Bear Mound is especially impressive: It's 137 feet long and 70 feet wide from shoulder to foreleg. *nps.gov/efmo*

FUN FACT

In 2020, wind energy accounted for 57% of the electricity supplied in Iowa— that's the largest share for any state.

NEARBY ATTRACTION

Iowa businessman Lowell Walter and his wife, Agnes, commissioned renowned architect Frank Lloyd Wright to build their dream home on a limestone bluff overlooking the Wapsipinicon River. One story high and 150 feet in length, Cedar Rock was built "green" and blends in with its natural surroundings. The home is now open to the public in Cedar Rock State Park, a gift of the Walter family to the Iowa State Conservation Commission. *exploreiowaparks .com*

▼

Effigy Mounds National Monument overlooks the Mississippi River.

I continued to follow the river, which twists and turns through valleys carved out of the distinctive landscape.

Once I reached New Albin, the state's northeasternmost city, I merged onto the Great River Road National Scenic Byway. Iowa's 328-mile section of the byway parallels the state line. Gigantic bluffs line the length of the Mississippi River into Wisconsin and Illinois, and farms dot the countryside.

During the winter, bald eagles flock to the open waters of the Mississippi. (The river doesn't freeze at the state's 11 locks and dams.) Between December and March, the bald eagle population in this area increases from 500 to 3,000, according to the Iowa Department of Natural Resources. That's when birds from neighboring states and Canada migrate here to fish.

If you want to see the majestic birds in action, consider taking advantage of the special events planned throughout January and February along Iowa's riverfront, including Eagle Watch and Cabin Fever Day in Guttenberg, about 58 miles from New Albin. A variety of charming river towns also offer good sightseeing locations.

Further south, in Lansing, you'll find panoramic views from Mount Hosmer Veteran's Memorial Park. Perched on a bluff 450 feet above the town, this park allows visitors to gaze out for miles into Wisconsin and boasts a stunning aerial view of the Mississippi riverbed below.

Between Lansing and Harpers Ferry, look for a lovely church nestled into the hills. Immaculate Conception Church at Wexford is said to be the oldest Catholic church between Dubuque, Iowa, and

St. Paul, Minnesota, and it still has a thriving congregation today.

Yellow River State Forest is a choice destination for outdoors enthusiasts. Visitors can spend the night in one of the camping cabins and take advantage of the many trails for horseback riding, cross-country skiing and hiking.

Effigy Mounds National Monument, a few miles north of Marquette, preserves more than 200 prehistoric mounds built by Native Americans of the Woodland culture. Numerous mounds there are shaped like bears and birds.

Fourteen miles of trails lead hikers past the ancient mounds and to scenic views of the Upper Mississippi River Valley. If you're lucky, you may spot a train or a barge moving cargo through the valley or the storied waters below.

Pikes Peak State Park, in McGregor, is one of the more popular destinations in this area, and for good reason. Here, a viewing platform on a 500-foot bluff allows you to see islands on the river, as well as Prairie du Chien, Wisconsin, across the border. You can also walk along a half-mile boardwalk to reach the stunning Bridal Veil Falls.

Finally, if you're journeying through this stretch of Iowa, a visit south to Balltown is essential. This was my last stop, and it did not disappoint. Scenic overlooks high above the land provide the quintessential Iowa view of pasture and farmsteads as far as the eye can see. Be sure to make a pit stop at Breitbach's Country Dining, a sixth-generation family-owned restaurant that happens to be Iowa's oldest eatery.

I returned home to Des Moines with confirmation that my beautiful state has plenty of opportunities for not only the adventure seeker, but the photographer as well, all within a few hundred miles. Maybe that line from the movie *Field of Dreams*, filmed not far from Balltown, in Dyersville, had it right:

"Is this Heaven?"

No. It's Iowa. ◼

▼
The sky, sun and moon loom large over Iowa's flatter regions.

Kansas

STORY AND PHOTOS BY
JENNIFER BROADSTREET HESS

ELK FALLS

SPEND A WEEKEND ADMIRING FUNKY VINTAGE CAMPERS.

THE VINTAGE CAMPER SHOW is one of the quirky highlights of the Outhouse Tour fall festival in Elk Falls, Kansas, which is held the last Friday and Saturday before Thanksgiving.

Hoping to beat the crowds, my friend Holly Bethe and I pulled into town right at sunrise. We found the trailers nestled in a lot just off the curving highway.

As we strolled through the lot, it was easy to see that these folks had put a lot of heart and time into remodeling their trailers. Exhibitors were eager to share stories of their campers' renovations and decor styles.

My favorite camper was built by Gale McCammon, an avid outdoorsman. He built his hunting cabin on the bed of his vintage pickup truck. Gale and his wife, Twila, decorated the camper with the comforts of home. A wood-burning stove kept the interior toasty, but my favorite feature was the inviting back porch. I imagined sitting a spell in the old-fashioned rocking chair to read or gaze up at the stars.

Another favorite was a classic Serro Scotty Sportsman trailer. This happy blue camper was adorned with plaid curtains on the windows and a brightly colored homemade quilt on the bed.

The interior was rehabbed with wood panels and chrome touches above the gas stove and in the kitchen area. Made for comfort and practicality, built-in shelving held necessary supplies for every road trip.

Vintage camper shows have become a form of rebellion in an era dominated by technology and fast-paced lifestyles. These trailers were constructed in the '40s, '50s and '60s, with affordability in mind. They remind us of a time when families would skip the interstate and travel America's back roads instead. Warm, fuzzy memories of camping at Melvern Lake with my best friend Vicki and her family in their vintage 1960s Shasta travel trailer come to mind. We floated down the road in their roomy green '76 Ford Crown Victoria, pulling a well-used but comfortable camper— no fancy bells or whistles.

Today, these lightweight glamping structures are popular with both the older and younger generations who admire them for their simplicity.

Vintage camper shows like the one in Elk Falls bring together people from all walks of life who have a love for these iconic works of art—and memorable stories to share. ●

Top: Gale McCammon's camper captures his personality. Bottom: The comforts of home make this interior cozy.

Points of INTEREST

NOT TO BE MISSED

Vintage campers aren't the only things worth touring in Elk Falls. Every fall, the town—the self-proclaimed outhouse capital of Kansas—hosts an Outhouse Tour and Contest. Visitors can pick up a ballot and judge 20 or so spruced-up outhouses in the area. You'll have plenty of stories to tell and, for a dollar, a commemorative button, too. *elkfallsouthouse tour.com*

SIDE TRIP

Head east from Elk Falls for about 90 miles and you'll find Big Brutus, the largest electric shovel in the world. The shovel, a Bucyrus Erie model 1850-B, looks like a creature designed for a science fiction movie. It stands 16 stories (160 feet) tall and weighs 11 million pounds. Visitors can climb five stories to the operator's compartment to get a great view. The visitors center offers picnic tables and comfort facilities complete with hot showers. *bigbrutus.org*

▼

As you approach Harbor Springs, take it slow and savor the autumn splendor along the M-119 scenic route.

STORY BY
JEANNE AMBROSE

TUNNEL OF TREES

TRAVEL UNDER A CANOPY OF COLOR ON THIS NORTHWEST
MICHIGAN SCENIC HERITAGE ROUTE.

THIS IS IT. This full-on fall drive through northern Michigan's Tunnel of Trees is so beautiful I just can't help but gush. It's breathtaking. Mesmerizing. Vivid. Branches thick with vibrant, colorful leaves drape artfully over the 20-plus-mile stretch of M-119 known as Tunnel of Trees Scenic Heritage Route. It's simply amazing.

The canopy of red-orange, yellow and gold leafy branches always transports me to a magical, peaceful place. Look up as bits of color drop from above and twirl down, carpeting the narrow road with leaves. Up ahead, you'll likely find that the sky is a brilliant blue. Glance to the side and you'll see either a dense forest of hardwoods and evergreens or a view of Lake Michigan from the bluffs.

Take your time here—the Tunnel of Trees, with its nearly 140 twisty curves and dips, is not for travelers in a hurry. Plus, along the way you'll want to stop and hike—or snowshoe—depending on the weather.

Most people begin their drive near Harbor Springs on Little Traverse Bay and head north through the tiny village of Good Hart (population about 600) on

their way to even tinier Cross Village (population not quite 300), the last stop along the Tunnel of Trees. But as fall and winter bump into each other, I like to start in the north and leisurely wend my way south. Fall's vivid colors can't be beat, and winter's isolated beauty brings peace and solitude.

Although you'll find that some tourist spots, lodging options and restaurants are closed for business from the end of October until spring, in late fall you can enjoy the scenery at your own pace without crowds or traffic jams.

That's why, as the temperatures drop, I take the quick route north via U.S. 31 or Interstate 75 and spend the night in Mackinaw City situated at the base of the Mackinac Bridge that connects the state's lower and upper peninsulas. From Mackinaw City it's only about 30 minutes to Cross Village and M-119. You'll be glad for every extra minute you have to spend exploring the hidden gems and wonders along this route.

If you're really taking the drive for an adventure, start at Wilderness State Park, about 5.5 miles north of Cross Village, and pitch a tent or sleep in a

Points of INTEREST

REST STOP

Cross Village's Legs Inn is a bizarre and fascinating restaurant decorated with taxidermic animals, carved totems and antlers. The spot serves up excellent Polish food and spectacular scenery. It is closed in the winter but is worth a visit during warmer months. *legsinn.com*

NOT TO BE MISSED

Find handcrafted artwork, hand-stamped linen Christmas stockings, tea towels, gorgeous artisan jewelry and Native American quill work at Three Pines Studio and Gallery. *threepinesstudio.com*

WORDS TO THE WISE

Wilderness State Park is a great place to observe meteor showers. Visit in mid-November for the Leonids meteor shower and mid-December for the Geminids. For more information about dark sky events in the area, visit *michigan.gov/dnr /places/state-parks /dark-sky-events.*

▼

Explore the charming shops that line Main Street in Harbor Springs.

rustic cabin or bunkhouse. To be clear, when I say rustic, I mean outhouses, pump-your-own water and bring-your-own flashlights because there is no electricity (except in the bunkhouses). Always come prepared!

I once spent a frosty winter weekend in Wilderness State Park with a group of friends and our cross-country skis and had an unforgettable time. The park, which encompasses more than 10,000 acres, is designated a dark-sky area, so tote along a reclining chair and bundle yourself up in a sleeping bag to gaze up at a sky unblemished by light pollution. Meteor showers in November and December—and the miles of trails for snowshoeing, cross-country skiing and hiking, along with 26 miles of Lake Michigan shoreline—make this a truly magical place to be.

After overnighting in the park, head south to Cross Village. Check out Three Pines Studio, a studio and gallery that features the work of local artists. (It's a

great place for Christmas shopping!) The day after Thanksgiving brings holiday cheer: There's a tree-lighting ceremony, chestnuts roasting over an open fire outside the studio and other family-friendly festivities.

As you head toward Good Hart, the halfway point along the route, watch for historical markers and be sure to take advantage of any pull-off parking spots. Take a few moments to absorb the views and the area's history.

I always make a stop at Good Hart General Store (which also serves as the post office). The atmosphere is homey and the potpies are glorious. Dine in or take them home to bake. Turkey potpie was recently added to the menu "in response to the notion that people were not traveling to visit family during the holidays," says Ami Woods, whose family has owned the store since 1971 when her mother purchased it from the original owner (who built it back in 1934).

With a full belly (or a full cooler), continue southward and watch for the Hoogland Family Nature Preserve. This 100-acre expanse will give you a great chance to stretch your legs. A 1.5-mile loop trail starts along a flat path through a forest of stately oak, birch and cedar trees. Soon the trail begins a steady ascent that may have you huffing and puffing by the time you reach the bluff. Once at the top, you'll have time to catch your breath as you take in the photoworthy, 360-degree view that includes Lake Michigan stretching to the horizon.

Or keep driving to Pond Hill Farm, a beacon that signifies you're nearing the end of your journey. Squeeze in a last outdoor adventure here—or wander through the livestock barn and market and grab a bite in the cafe. This stop is a great option for families, especially during the holidays.

Thanksgiving weekend on Pond Hill Farm includes Christmas cookies, wreath decorating, ornament making and, pandemic allowing, a visit from Santa. Marci Spencer, one of the farm's owners, says, "In the winter, we offer groomed trails for cross-country skiing, snowshoeing, hiking or fat-tire biking, with a gnome-house hunt throughout the trails. We also have a sledding hill down the vineyard, specialty hot cocoas, and wine, beer and cider tasting."

Hit the road for the last stretch and make a final stop in Harbor Springs—it's a charming little city surrounded by beauty and a lovely place to emerge from the Tunnel of Trees and re-enter the real world. If I'm hungry, I'll stop at Stafford's Pier Restaurant and claim a table near the window overlooking the bay. I'll relax, relive the day's adventure and stretch out the trip with a bit of delicious joy: oak-planked whitefish and, if it's on the menu, morel bisque. Although, I'll also be anxious to get back home and bake the turkey potpie I picked up along the way. ●

▼
Pick the perfect pumpkin or squash at Pond Hill Farm.

Minnesota

STORY AND PHOTO BY
ANGIE SABO

CALEDONIA

JOURNEY TO THE HEART OF BARN QUILT COUNTRY.

IN THE HILLS and valleys of Caledonia, Minnesota, dusty gravel roads traverse acres of soybeans, corn and alfalfa. The prairie is covered with red clover, pale purple field thistle and Queen Anne's lace—it's quite a treat for the eyes.

But for a real adventure, behold the weathered barns. High up on those walls you'll see colorful painted quilt blocks in patterns such as Maple Leaf, Sunbonnet Sue and Gentleman's Fancy, to name a few. The quilt blocks were installed on barns in Caledonia in 2007 as a way to preserve the area's rural heritage. At that time, Minnesota was losing around 1,400 barns per year.

You'll be able to see about 60 barn quilts in the region; you can download a handy map at *caledoniamn.gov* (enter "barn quilt" in the search bar).

After photographing a red barn, I sat in the grass and imagined a farmer at work, milking the cows and loading hay into the loft. Days working on a farm are long and hard, but most farmers would not trade them for a job in a city.

Rural America has so much to offer the senses. Come out and experience it. Spending a day in clean air and open spaces connects us to the traditions, history and beauty of country life. ●

Quilt block art adds a pop of color to barns in Caledonia.

STORY BY
JO-ELLEN WILLIS

HANNIBAL

CRUISE INTO LITERARY HISTORY.

SAMUEL CLEMENS, better known by his pen name, Mark Twain, was raised in Hannibal, Missouri, on the banks of the Mississippi River. His childhood home, which is now open to the public, is a charming two-story cottage with shuttered windows. The white garden fence along its side yard likely provided the inspiration for the character Tom Sawyer conniving to have his friends whitewash fence boards for him.

Inside, historical treasures await: Twain's pipe, writing desk and chair and first editions of his novels. The home provides visitors with a colorful glimpse into the early life that inspired many of Twain's best-loved tales.

During my visit to Hannibal, I took a relaxing two-hour cruise along the Mississippi River on the Mark Twain Riverboat. The sound of the steam whistle, the ring of the large bell and the sight of cotton bales stacked along the decks animated thoughts of the passengers Twain described in his writing: cotton traders, politicians, miners, gunslingers and gamblers.

Delving into Twain's early life was a fascinating counterpart to reading his work. It sparked my imagination and stretched my mind. ✺

▼

The Mark Twain Boyhood Home & Museum is open for tours.

▼
Bison calves get to know the herd and the prairie at the Fort Niobrara National Wildlife Refuge in Valentine.

STORY AND PHOTOS BY
CHUCK HANEY

SANDHILLS

DRIVE OR BIKE BENEATH AN OPEN SKY ACROSS PLAINS CUT BY THE MIGHTY NIOBRARA RIVER.

AS A LANDSCAPE PHOTOGRAPHER, I am often asked what is my favorite ecosystem to shoot. My answer? The Great Plains. That fact often comes as a surprise to my inquirer, but it shouldn't. Here in this uncrowded landscape, the sky is dominant. Storms are dramatic and abrupt, and the vast grasslands teem with wildlife.

My go-to Great Plains destination is the Sandhills area of north-central Nebraska, a region of sprawling sand dunes that were declared a National Natural Landmark in 1984. Here, the hills can reach heights of more than 400 feet, but what most distinguishes this region from other sandy areas are the flourishing grasses, which include bluestem, sand lovegrass and prairie sand reed varieties. Their roots form the fabric that holds the dunes in place, and without them, the sands would be swept away by the wind.

A few scenic byways go through this area. Whenever I get a chance to visit,

I like to customize my trip by devising a loop that combines the best parts of the region into a grand tour.

I begin my journey in the small town of Valentine. A plethora of red street signs emblazoned with hearts give this town a charming and whimsical feel. Each year around 5,000 romantics send their Valentine's Day cards through the local post office in order to receive that year's Valentine postmark.

After spending a bit of time getting reacquainted with the town, I explore nearby attractions like Fort Niobrara National Wildlife Refuge. Situated on more than 19,000 acres straddling the Niobrara, a National Scenic River, the refuge boasts a diverse grassland habitat that supports bison, elk and deer herds along with myriad smaller prairie mammals and bird species. I particularly enjoy driving through the complex on the auto tour route just as the sun rises. The ride is special in late spring, when the bison herd swells with

Points of INTEREST

NOT TO BE MISSED

The arrival of the sandhill cranes each spring brings birders to this area from across the country. The Nebraska Crane Festival is a monthlong celebration of their arrival. Visit the Rowe Sanctuary for tours, viewings and seminars. *ne.audubon.org /crane-festival*

WORDS TO THE WISE

If you'll be touring by bicycle, start early in the day before the wind picks up speed and the heat kicks in. Bring a repair kit with you, stay hydrated, and last but not least, have a camera ready!

NEARBY ATTRACTION

When the greater prairie chicken does its mating dance, birders head to Calamus Outfitters on the Switzer Ranch. In addition to offering safari-style birding tours, the Switzer family hosts the Nebraska Prairie-Chicken Festival every other year. The ranch also hosts eco-tours of the grassland and river trips. *calamusoutfitters .com*

▼

Grab a bite or snap a photo at the historic general store in Meadville.

newborn calves. This always evokes a "wow" moment under the canopy of the big open sky. And there are birding opportunities within the refuge, plus hiking trails that lead to a waterfall.

Visitors to Valentine can also rent an inner tube or a canoe to float along the Niobrara River. Many outfitters in town will drop you off and then shuttle you back after a few hours of relaxation on the lazily flowing river.

I head out of Valentine going east on Highway 12, also known as the Outlaw Trail Scenic Byway. The road makes its way east for 231 miles, all the way to the Iowa border in Sioux City. When I recently toured part of the route by bicycle, I was impressed by the friendly waves from the few passing pickup trucks, whose cabs mostly contained silhouetted outlines of cowboy hats.

Nebraska is known as the Cornhusker State, but in the Sandhills there are far more cattle ranches and open grassland areas than cornfields.

I could soon see why the byway got its moniker. The steep bluffs and forested canyons of the Niobrara River Valley would have been choice hiding places in the late 1800s for horse thieves like Doc Middleton and his Pony Boys. Even notorious bank robbers such as Jesse James were rumored to have holed up in this region's natural hiding spots.

Smith Falls State Park, Nebraska's newest park and home to its highest waterfall, is a hidden gem and just a quick detour south of Highway 12. A short footbridge and nature trail lead to a viewing platform where you can watch the water gently descend over a 63-foot-tall cliff. The park is also a popular stop for folks canoeing the Niobrara River. There is tent camping, a shower facility and a picnic area at the site.

Just west of the small village of Springview lies Cub Creek Recreation Area, where a small lake is popular for birding, fishing, paddling and camping. The area also sees spectacular sunrises and sunsets. While camping there, I awoke, exited my tent and found a fiery sky perfectly reflecting on the lake's calm surface—simply breathtaking.

South of Highway 12, Meadville Road leads to a ghost town of the same name. This isn't off-roading because the route is a rather well-maintained gravel road. A bridge crosses the Niobrara River at a wide and handsome spot. There is a historic general store and post office in Meadville that is open sporadically. Exploring the small towns in the heart of the Sandhills is a must.

About 15 miles south of Meadville, I headed east on Highway 20 then north on Highway 7 to the Bassett Lodge and Range Cafe. The diner features a tasty breakfast and lunch menu that refuels me for more miles when I'm riding my bike on a nearby rail trail. The sizable cattle drive photo over the counter and rustic decor give a real local flavor. The lodge has been around since 1949, and the lobby's antique motif transports you back to a time when cattle buyers from all across the United States were drawn to the town's sale barn.

If I am traveling earlier in the spring, I trek south of Bassett on Highways 183 and 96 to visit the Switzer Ranch and Calamus Outfitters and take advantage of their birding tours. Observing and photographing greater prairie chickens and sharp-tailed grouse from a blind is a real treat for me. In the summer, you can float the Calamus River right from the ranch and beat the Nebraska heat and humidity.

When driving back toward Valentine on Highway 20, you'll spot an adjacent

▼

Long Pine Creek carves its way through the area.

▼

Nebraska's newest state park, Smith Falls, features its highest cascade.

▼
Cycling across this trestle on the Cowboy Trail affords impressive views of the Niobrara River.

rail trail. The 195-mile Cowboy Trail is a converted railbed that follows the former Chicago & North Western Railway lines across the state from Norfolk all the way to Valentine.

The recreational trail is shared by hikers, horseback riders and bicyclists. I pedaled the section from Bassett to Valentine. Cycling was an intimate way to experience the Sandhills region as I stopped at small towns, visited with locals and had the thrill of rolling across two large trestles. The Long Pine Trestle is 145 feet high and spans Long Pine Creek; Valentine's grand trestle extends over the Niobrara River at 148 feet high and is a quarter of a mile long. It was an exciting ride with wonderful views.

Upon returning to Valentine, I took one more detour from my Sandhills loop: I exited Highway 20 just east of Valentine to drive south on Highway 83 to the Valentine National Wildlife Refuge. This 72,000-acre refuge protects one of the largest remaining tracts of tallgrass and mixed-grass prairie habitat in the country. White pelicans, upland sandpipers and long-billed curlews are among the birds likely to be seen here.

In this area, the rolling hills are accented by numerous old-fashioned windmills that draw water from the underground Ogallala Aquifer. Shallow lakes and wetlands are also created as fresh, ancient water seeps up from the aquifer. I love driving slowly around the refuge's dirt roads looking for birds and wildlife.

Journeying through the Nebraska Sandhills on a grand tour takes me to a place where the pace is slower and troubles seem fewer. ✦

STORY AND PHOTO BY
RONALD KINGSLEY

CASSELTON

FIVE NORTH DAKOTA GOVERNORS HAIL FROM THIS TOWN WITH CLOSE TIES TO NORTH DAKOTA HISTORY AND HERITAGE.

ST. STEPHEN'S EPISCOPAL CHURCH was built in 1886 in the town of Casselton, North Dakota, by Gen. George Washington Cass Jr. A respected industrialist and former president of the Northern Pacific Railway, Cass built the church to thank the locals for naming the town in his honor.

Rocks were shipped to Casselton by train from a nearby town and hauled to the site by Red River carts. The church was built in the Gothic Revival style, with pointed arches, a tall steeple and 18 lovely stained-glass windows, which were reportedly made in France.

The shipping address—St. Stephen's Church, Dakota Territory—is inscribed on the back of one of the pews. The bell in the steeple tower, smelted in London, is inscribed, "In memory of George Cass Jr."

In 1951 the church was placed on the market because the congregation was dwindling and the building was in need of several repairs. Local Mennonites looking for a church home paid $3,500 for it. Their improvements, such as repairing the round window to hold the glass in place, helped save the church from deterioration.

When the Mennonite congregation disbanded in 2004, Twila Schrock, the daughter of former pastor Abe Stoll, organized a group of local volunteers to preserve the church and acquire historic documents from the area. Now called the Casselton Heritage Center, the building is available for weddings, funerals and other gatherings.

The library is dedicated to five North Dakota governors from the Casselton area, with photos and memorabilia portraying their political and personal lives. The center also has a display by local artists and a collection of pictures, yearbooks and documents depicting the early days of the community.

The Casselton Heritage Center is open to the public during Casselton Community Days in July and other special events, or by appointment.

Volunteers are always willing to show folks around and help them research their ancestry. Last summer, visitors came to the Casselton Heritage Center all the way from Canada, Australia and New Zealand.

To learn more about local history or schedule a tour, visit *casselton.com /casselton-heritage-center*. ●

REST STOP

For some local flavor, pay a visit to 4e Winery in nearby Mapleton. Run by Greg and Lisa Cook, the winery offers a wide selection of wines—including Prairie Breeze and Rail Line Red—made locally from prairie ingredients. Enjoy a glass and some light bites on the outdoor deck. *4ewinery.com*

NEARBY ATTRACTION

Bagg Bonanza Historical Farm, in Mooreton, offers fascinating insights into the life of a 19th-century megafarm. In the 1870s, "bonanza" farms of 30,000 acres and more (among the largest in the world) sprang up in North Dakota after the financial collapse of the Northern Pacific Railway. Investors took land in place of worthless rail bonds and sold vast stretches to men like J. F. Downing, a Pennsylvania lawyer. Downing's nephew F.A. Bagg managed the 5,000-acre farm.

▼

The former church has 18 gorgeous stained-glass windows.

Netcher Road Covered Bridge, built in 1998, is a single-span bridge of neo-Victorian design.

Ohio

STORY BY
TONYA PRATER

ASHTABULA COUNTY

SEEK OUT CENTURIES-OLD COVERED BRIDGES IN THE
NORTHEASTERN CORNER OF THE BUCKEYE STATE.

OHIO HAS MORE covered bridges than nearly any other state in the country. The "covered bridge capital of Ohio," Ashtabula County, boasts 19 covered bridges—with 17 of them drivable—including America's longest and shortest covered bridges. You can thank the skilled woodworkers for crafting structures that have endured the elements and the test of time—in some cases, more than 100 years. But even more surprising is that these aren't all historic structures; some of these bridges were built in the 21st century. My husband, Rod, and I spent a day seeking out a few of our favorites. They are equally beautiful against the splendid backdrop of fall foliage or blanketed in winter's new fallen snow.

Starting from The Lodge at Geneva-on-the-Lake, we headed south on State Route 534 toward the town of Geneva and the West Liberty Street Covered Bridge. America's shortest covered bridge, at only 18 feet, has an unusual open structure that was built using modular components by students from the Ashtabula County Joint Vocational

School. You'll find plentiful parking as well as an information booth at this one-of-a-kind structure.

A few miles south of the West Liberty Street Covered Bridge, we stopped at the Harpersfield Covered Bridge, which is the second-longest covered bridge in Ohio and spans the Grand River. When the soil at one end of the bridge was washed away during the Great Dayton Flood of 1913, a steel section was added, making this a unique structure to drive through. The adjacent park offers opportunities for birding, picnicking, kayaking and more on its 53 acres.

Heading east, we soon arrived at the Mechanicsville Road Covered Bridge. Built in 1867 and renovated in 2003, the bridge is listed on the National Register of Historic Places and is considered the oldest covered bridge in the southern part of the county. It is also the longest single-span bridge in the county.

Traveling along the heavily tree-lined Mechanicsville Road, you'll spot the white bridge with the red metal roof at the junction with Orchardgrove Drive. Note the barn-quilt square on the side

Points of INTEREST

REST STOPS

Across the street from Mechanicsville Road Covered Bridge is the Grand River Manor, the oldest tavern in county. The bar dates to 1847 and is a popular stop for those on the covered bridge tour. Order a burger and nab a seat on the outside patio overlooking the river. *facebook.com/grand rivermanor*

The area around Geneva is known for its wineries. Dine in Geneva's historic Old Mill Winery and try one of the signature wine burgers. *theoldmillwinery.com*

WORDS TO THE WISE

Plan to view the sunset on Lake Erie at the beach area in Geneva State Park. During warmer months, this location is a popular spot to search for beach glass. *ohiodnr.gov*

NEARBY ATTRACTION

Visit Olin's Museum of Covered Bridges in Ashtabula to learn about the rich heritage of Ashtabula County and its bridges. *coveredbridge museum.org*

Ashtabula County has 19 covered bridges, including the Smolen-Gulf.

of the bridge. There are more than 100 such squares throughout the county, but only three appear on covered bridges. Just ahead and to the left of the bridge, you can pull off the road to get a closer look.

Follow the meandering back roads east through the countryside to nearby Jefferson and find four more bridges. The Giddings Road, South Denmark Road, Doyle Road and Netcher Road covered bridges all span Mill Creek, a tributary of the Grand River. Netcher Road was of particular interest to me. The red-and-white bridge features a distinct neo-Victorian design unlike any other bridge on the route. A small gravel pull-off allows motorists to get off the road and walk through the bridge for a closer look and scenic photo-op.

We then made our way northeast to the Smolen-Gulf Covered Bridge, built in 2008. The longest covered bridge in the United States, it stretches 613 feet and sits 93 feet above the Ashtabula

River in Indian Trails Park. Rod and I parked and made our way along the highway toward the bridge to admire it on foot since there's a handy sidewalk.

From the bridge, we could hear the river's running water. We peered over the handrails to get a glimpse of the county's newest covered bridge less than 400 feet away—the Riverview Covered Bridge. Built in 2016, the Riverview is a pedestrian bridge modeled after the Smolen-Gulf. It's another perfect spot to pause and take in the scenery.

Viewing the historic covered bridges in Ashtabula County transported me to the carefree days of my childhood when my family would pile into our 1970-something Dodge Aspen and traverse the back roads of the state. The difference between this trip and those childhood trips that took place many years ago? I've finally grown to appreciate how magical the remnants of yesteryear can truly be. ❧

South Dakota

STORY BY
KATHLEEN UNGERER

BLACK HILLS

IN SOUTH DAKOTA'S BLACK HILLS, VIEWS ASTOUND AND
NATURE IS ALL AROUND.

WE ALL HAVE special places that we return to time and again. When these places call to us, we must go. For me, one of those places is the Black Hills of South Dakota. Many scenic drives traverse this mountain range. So on a gorgeous day, I set off on a three-day road trip.

On the first day, I head toward the impressive Iron Mountain Road. In no time at all, I reach the architectural wonder of the wooden pigtail bridges and know I'm on the great road itself, which boasts 17 miles of twists and turns, jaw-dropping vistas and narrow tunnels that perfectly frame Mount Rushmore. The switchbacks and sights along this awe-inspiring road demand that I slow down for a moment and just behold the world around me.

Later, I make my way into Custer State Park and drive onto the 18-mile

▼
Custer State Park's annual buffalo roundup is a sight to behold.

BLAINE HARRINGTON III/GETTY IMAGES

Points of INTEREST

REST STOP

Hill City's historic Alpine Inn restaurant features a simple menu inspired by European cuisine. Savor a bacon-wrapped filet mignon, a huge wedge salad and a baked potato for an affordable price. *alpineinnhillcity.com*

SIDE TRIP

Rapid City, a gateway town to the Black Hills, still has an Old West feel with plenty of original buildings and a thriving art and entertainment community.

NEARBY ATTRACTIONS

Soothe your senses in the Jon Crane Gallery, an art gallery showcasing Jon Crane's stunning watercolors depicting scenes of South Dakota life. Works of other local artists are also on display. *joncranegallery.net*

From June to August, the Black Hills Playhouse just off Needles Highway stages top-notch productions. A Custer State Park Pass is required to see the shows. *blackhillsplayhouse.com*

▼

The 1880 Train heads into the heart of the Black Hills.

Wildlife Loop. Although I've been here many times, I can't resist the chance to see bison, pronghorns, bighorn sheep, mule deer, prairie dogs and the very friendly wild burros always begging for attention. It's no wonder these hills were once the hunting grounds of the Sioux people.

My route soon takes me up and over Mount Coolidge to the historic State Game Lodge, a beautiful native stone and wood structure that was once the summer White House of President Calvin Coolidge. I end my day here with a satisfying dinner and then sit back in a rocking chair on the front porch, where I watch a bison stroll by on the front lawn.

I start the next day bright and early because I want to snag a ticket for the Buffalo Safari Jeep Tour, which gets up close to bison and other wildlife. The driver takes our group over rough terrain and maneuvers us so that we are surrounded by bison that show no interest in us at all. I could practically reach out and touch them.

Our very capable guide then asks if we want to go off-off-roading, and that's where the rocks and mud come in. The exhilarating, bumpy trek feels like a real adventure and takes place just up the road from the lodge.

After the safari, we set out to explore Needles Highway, so named because it winds through needle-like granite formations. This is a white-knuckled, nail-biting, heart-pounding ride to the Eye of the Needle. I jostle for space to take a photo and cringe when I see a tour bus squeezing through the tunnel at the top. The view is spectacular and scary at the same time.

At the end, I'm happy to reach the idyllic Sylvan Lake, which I've often said is my favorite place on earth. The deep blue water surrounded by giant boulders is an absolutely dazzling sight. After hiking around the lake— a challenging three-mile trail leads to the summit of Harney Peak and sweeping views of the nearby Black Elk Wilderness Area—I take some time to relax in a cozy cabin.

On the final day of my trip, I stop in Hill City, an old gold-rush town, to ride the steam-powered 1880 Train, which once carried mined gold. Now the train is a beloved piece of history, chugging past Tin Mill Hill, Good Luck Tungsten Mine, Black Elk Peak, Battle Creek Falls, Elkhorn Mountain and Old Baldy Mountain, just as it did in the Old West.

When I say goodbye to the Black Hills, I am sad to leave. But soon the Hills will call to me again and I will go. It's my heaven on earth. ❧

Granite spires ◄
attract hikers and
climbers to Custer
State Park.

▼
Horses pulling Amish buggies are a common sight in Wisconsin's Driftless Region.

STORY AND PHOTOS BY
BOB FIRTH

AMISH COUNTRY

COME ALONG WITH PHOTOGRAPHER BOB FIRTH ON
A SCENIC CIRCLE TOUR OF SOUTHWESTERN WISCONSIN.

IF A LANDSCAPE could be described in terms of a musical style, southwestern Wisconsin's Amish country would surely be classical.

Undulating country hills flow like notes on a scale, rising and falling in a soothing symphony of visual music. The solid, percussive sound of horses' clopping feet creates a steady rhythm indicative of the simple life of those living here.

In my experience, the best way to immerse yourself in this mosaic of farmland, woodlands and streams along the awe-inspiring Mississippi River is to drive through it. Over the years, I've followed a meandering 100-mile loop tour that allows for spur-of-the-moment stops in quaint towns and at antique stores, farmers markets and country shops selling homemade Amish foods and crafts of all kinds. While I've mapped out my preferred route, I encourage you to craft one of your own. Follow your instincts and the hand-painted signs

to experience an unforgettable adventure that's just right for you.

My ideal journey starts in the city of La Crosse at the Mississippi River and moves south on state Highway 35. Continuing onto U.S. Highway 14/61 brings you toward Coon Valley, a lovely little town that marks the gateway to Amish country.

Pop in to Valley Market and stock up on snacks, or grab a bite at the rustic Stockyard Grill & Saloon. Then wend your way to Westby, the agricultural hub of the area. Stretch your legs with a leisurely walk down the old Main Street as you take in the many historic buildings and churches.

From Westby, drive north on state Highway 27 to Cashton, then take state Highway 33 east and head south on County Road D. This is the true heart of Amish country. Watching the men work the fields with horse-drawn plows and haying equipment is impressive and inspiring. Forests, fields and fences blend like the stitching on a quilt.

Points of INTEREST

WORDS TO THE WISE

All Amish shops, farms and places of business are closed on Sundays.

Plan to use cash if you want to purchase goods or services. Most Amish businesses do not accept credit cards.

Use caution when driving over hills or passing vehicles, because of horse-drawn buggies. Avoid parking on hills or pulling over near them.

Respect the privacy and beliefs of the Amish. Their religion forbids posing for photos, especially those showing their faces. Keep your cellphones and cameras at a distance.

NEARBY ATTRACTION

A quick detour 10 miles east of Cashton on state Highway 33 brings you to Ontario, the "canoe capital of the Kickapoo." Famous for its beauty and easy canoeing, the Kickapoo River is an ideal spot to indulge in a one- to three-hour fully supplied canoe trip arranged by one of several outfitters in the area.

▼

Amish children race to school wearing traditional garb.

The countryside is beautiful here in a quiet sort of way, and the roads offer spectacular open scenic views. This is the Driftless Area of Wisconsin's Mississippi River Valley. The region's characteristic landscape results from its good fortune in being bypassed by the last continental glacier.

At times what you see feels a bit like a Norman Rockwell painting. Rolling hills and farm after farm with hand-painted signs beckon you to stop and purchase Amish wares. Follow your impulses and detour from the loop with side trips that interest you. One of the wonderful parts of this trip is shopping directly from the Amish on their farms.

Often a long driveway will lead you to a simple stand or small outbuilding where Amish women and girls mind the stores. There you'll find homemade jams, maple syrup, jellies, chocolates, candy, honey, eggs, fresh fruits and just-picked vegetables.

Be sure to visit the in-home Amish bakeries with wonderful breads, rolls and more. My favorite stop off County Road D is the Sunrise Bakery near Bloomingdale for its amazing baked goods. Meeting the people and doing business with them is delightful—a cultural exchange you will cherish long after your visit has come to an end.

Amish women are also known for their beautiful quilts, rugs, hats, socks, mittens and other textiles. Along the way I like to buy homemade one-of-a-kind items for Christmas gifts.

Amish furniture, handmade from local wood by men at the pinnacle of craftsmanship, is available throughout the area. One can find many treasures, from wooden toys to sheds to sturdy indoor and outdoor furniture. For the

Amish, woodworking is a skill passed down over generations. Amish beliefs forbid the use of the electrical grid, so many shop tools are powered by hydraulics or pneumatic systems run by diesel generators.

Once County Road D zigzags its way south to Highway 82, head west to Viroqua, one of the largest towns on the loop drive and the best place for gas, lodging and food. Stop in at the Viroqua Food co-op for natural, locally grown organic goods. Visit the Historic Temple Theatre, built in 1922, and take in some live music, comedy, theater or a film. Plan your trip so you can eat at one of the restaurants in Viroqua and you won't be disappointed.

The towering rocky bluffs that signal the Mississippi River Valley lie west of Viroqua on state Highway 56. Head through the hills toward Genoa, a small town on the river. Stop and visit Lock and Dam 8 on the south end of this town for an up-close view of boats and barges as they pass up and down the river. Rustic Genoa Motel, the only hotel in town, is just across the road from the river.

As you travel shoulder to shoulder along the Mississippi River, you'll enjoy panoramic vistas of the river valley and bluffs as you head north on state Highway 35 through Stoddard back toward La Crosse. If you time it right, looking west over the Mississippi at sunset rewards you with amazing views.

You could drive this trip in a few hours. But those who have more time and an adventurous spirit could easily spend two or more days exploring this area. Just follow your instincts, your nose and the Amish signs. Venture off the loop drive and you'll find yourself zigzagging through the countryside along rustic roads as you navigate your way back again. This is a good place to get lost. And getting lost can be a good thing, because it takes you to places you've never been. ❧

▼
Wildcat Mountain State Park in Ontario offers picturesque views.

The Harpersfield Covered Bridge, built in 1868, stretches across the Grand River in Ohio.

"Let me recommend the best medicine in the world: a long journey, at a mild season, through a pleasant country, in easy stages."

—JAMES MADISON

SOUTHEAST

▼

The view of Little River Canyon from Wolf Creek Overlook dazzles, aglow with leaves in fall hues.

STORY AND PHOTOS BY
PAT & CHUCK BLACKLEY

APPALACHIAN HIGHLANDS

REVEL IN THE SURPRISING FALL COLOR AND LEGENDARY HOSPITALITY IN ALABAMA'S APPALACHIAN HIGHLANDS.

WHEN PLANNING a fall leaf-peeping trip, Alabama may not immediately spring to mind. That's where you go for warm Gulf breezes wafting through the palm trees, right? Right.

But in Alabama's northern highlands you'll also find crisp, clear fall days and stunning mountain vistas wrapped in vivid foliage. The southern escarpment of the Appalachian Mountains rises from the Piedmont Plateau north of Birmingham and stretches across the state's northeast corner in waves of hardwood forest. In the fall, dogwoods, maples, golden poplars and hickories put on an extravagant show of color.

Several popular scenic roadways roam through these ancient mountains, including the Talladega Scenic Drive, Appalachian Highlands Scenic Byway and Lookout Mountain Parkway. But we also like getting out of the car and stretching our legs, so we planned our trip around four parks known for their hiking paths as well as their fall color.

DeSoto State Park near Fort Payne is a breathtaking resort park perched atop Lookout Mountain. Home to the Cherokee before the Trail of Tears, the park takes its name from Spanish conquistador Hernando de Soto, who is thought to have explored here while searching for gold in 1540. In the 1930s, the Civilian Conservation Corps, or CCC, developed the park. Many of the original CCC structures still stand, including the main part of DeSoto's Lodge, which is now the DeSoto State Park Mountain Inn Restaurant. The park also has a motel, rustic log cabins, A-frame chalets, a campground, a nature center and a CCC museum.

We, of course, were impressed with the 25-plus miles of hiking trails that took us through vividly colored forest, along the West Fork of Little River and

Points of INTEREST

REST STOP

Housed within a 1930s sandstone lodge built by the Civilian Conservation Corps, the Mountain Inn Restaurant in DeSoto State Park is a great place to enjoy a hot breakfast before embarking on a hike. *alapark.com /desoto-mountain -inn-restaurant*

NEARBY ATTRACTION

Russell Cave National Monument, in Bridgeport, is home to one of the oldest sites of human habitation in North America. A short, scenic boardwalk leads visitors to the ballroom-size cavern and allows them to imagine what it must have been like for Native Americans to shelter here thousands of years ago. A small museum at the visitors center displays weapon points and other tools found at the site. *nps.gov/ruca*

▼

A trail leads hikers to Pulpit Rock in Cheaha State Park.

past rock formations, waterfalls and rare plant life. The ADA-accessible Talmadge Butler Boardwalk Trail lets people of all abilities enjoy an intimate trip through brilliant foliage to a deck overlooking Azalea Cascade waterfall.

North of the inn, beautiful DeSoto Falls plunges 104 feet into a mountain lake rimmed with rocks. The area is one of the most photographed spots in Alabama. Above the falls, entrepreneur A.A. Miller built a hydroelectric dam to supply power to Fort Payne in the 1920s. Today, park visitors can fish, swim and canoe on the dam's lake.

Just a 15-minute drive south, we find Little River Canyon National Preserve. Little River runs 30 miles along the top of Lookout Mountain before flowing into Weiss Lake, making it the nation's longest mountaintop river. Along the way, it has carved one of the longest, deepest and most scenic gorge systems east of the Mississippi River.

Little River Canyon Scenic Drive (State Highway 176) follows the west rim for 11 miles. Eight overlooks offer views into the canyon, which plunges to depths of more than 600 feet. Some overlooks provide picnic spots and access to hiking trails. For a grand view of the 45-foot Little River Falls, stop at the northernmost overlook. In autumn, the water levels drop, but it is still a beautiful sight to behold.

Cheaha Resort State Park on Cheaha Mountain also earned a spot on our Alabama fall color must-see list. We visited during peak color season in late October, and the woods were ablaze with fiery red and orange maple trees.

Located south of Anniston on the Talladega Scenic Drive, this mountain got its name from the Creek Indians, who called it Chaha, or "high place." Bunker Fire Lookout Tower, built of native stone in the 1930s by the CCC, sits on the mountain's highest point, which is also the highest point in the state at about 2,400 feet.

Cheaha amenities include a lodge, a restaurant, chalets and a campground. Two hiking trails, Pulpit Rock and Rock Garden, lead to fabulous vistas of the Talladega National Forest's pristine wilderness. The wheelchair-accessible Bald Rock Trail meanders through scattered boulders and woods to a picturesque overlook at Bald Rock.

The area also offers access to several popular trails through the surrounding national forest, including the Kentuck ORV Trail for wheeled vehicles and the Pinhoti Trail, which connects with the Appalachian Trail.

Our last stop was Lake Guntersville State Park. This large resort park sits atop Taylor Mountain and overlooks the massive Lake Guntersville. The park features chalets and cabins; a restaurant, campground, 18-hole golf course and beach complex; boating and fishing; and 36 miles of hiking and biking trails that wind through almost 6,000 acres of woodlands.

The park's gorgeous lodge, perched on a high bluff overlooking the lake, features exposed wooden beams and stone fireplaces. Views from the back decks are spectacular, especially at sunrise and sunset.

In addition to the beauty of these mountains, the warm, friendly people we met here make this a truly special place. They love where they live and are eager to share stories and suggest special places to see. And the food! We found delicious down-home cooking everywhere we went—including the best fried chicken and banana pudding we've ever eaten.

After taking in its autumn charm, we have officially added the Alabama highlands to our list of favorite fall treks. We're already looking forward to our next chance to hike the trails as the fall breeze gently blows and fall's color show begins. ✿

▼
A rustic bridge in DeSoto State Park passes over Indian Falls.

STORY BY
DANA MEREDITH

MONAH

ANCIENT ARTIFACTS TELL THE STORY OF AMERICA'S
FIRST PEOPLE.

THE MUSEUM OF Native American History, or MONAH, in Bentonville, Arkansas, was included in *USA Today*'s Top 10 Best History Museums list in 2020 and 2021. The brainchild of creator and chairman David Bogle, a member of the Cherokee Nation, MONAH houses David's extensive private collection—along with other loaned and donated items—in exhibits of more than 10,000 of the finest Native American artifacts. The preserved skeleton of a woolly mammoth fondly known as Tusker greets visitors at the door.

The museum's mission is to educate future generations about those who first left their footprints on American soil and to raise awareness of the Native American communities making a difference today.

Free self-guided audio tours lead guests through displays of decorated clothing, tools, knives, Quapaw pottery and other treasures curated from across five time periods covering 14,000 years.

Wander the Indigenous Medicine Garden outdoors, or participate in the numerous free events and seminars held throughout the year. Five percent of the sales from books, pottery, toys, jewelry, art prints and collectibles in the online trading post directly benefits the Partnership of Native Americans. Admission to the museum is free, but the history you'll learn and the fun to be had are priceless. ●

Points of INTEREST

FUN FACT

Tusker, the woolly mammoth serving as the museum's "door greeter," was assembled using bones from three separate mammoths.

WORDS TO THE WISE

The museum is closed on Sundays. Check for hours and a schedule of events at *monah.org*.

SIDE TRIP

Eureka Springs, about an hour east of MONAH, has long been renowned for its legendary waters, which were once believed to have healing properties. The town was built up during the Victorian era and still boasts incredible original architecture from the period. The town has numerous art and antiques shops; offers garden, cave and ghost tours; and puts on the annual Great Passion Play, an outdoor event that draws big crowds in the summer. *eurekasprings.org*

Top: Hunt for arrowheads on the Museum of Native American History grounds. Bottom: The exhibits include ancient pottery, shown here with museum founder David Bogle.

TOP: MUSEUM OF NATIVE AMERICAN HISTORY; BOTTOM: MATT ROWE

Beachgoers relax in the sun and sand or search for seashells on Sanibel Island.

STORY AND PHOTOS BY
CHUCK HANEY

SANIBEL AND BEYOND

PHOTOGRAPHER CHUCK HANEY LEAVES SNOWY MONTANA AND
FLIES SOUTH TO SUNNY FLORIDA.

EACH FEBRUARY, my Ohio parents trade cold midwestern winters for southern Florida's tropical climate and pristine beaches. For years these snowbirds tried to convince me, a nature-loving photographer, to visit.

I hesitated because I didn't want to miss a ski day back home in Montana, and I was wary of the overcrowded urban sprawl that I imagined prevails in the Sunshine State.

Eventually I relented, and have since become a Florida fixture for several weeks each winter—a mini-snowbird, if you will. I've discovered that I can have a break from winter and satisfy my desire for nature because there are myriad natural wonders that can only be found in South Florida. The wildlife viewing and birding opportunities, as well as the unique and exotic (to this Montanan) ecosystem, won me over in the end.

My wife and I usually begin our stay on Sanibel Island, visiting family and relaxing on the beach, and then head south on a road trip to explore the Everglades and the Keys.

Sanibel Island's broad, white sandy beaches attract visitors from all over looking for fantastic sunsets and a break from the hectic pace of modern life. The beaches are well known for the seashells that wash up from the Gulf of Mexico with each tide. I love the fact that the condensed island has cycling trails that lead from our condo to J.N. Ding Darling National Wildlife Refuge. The sanctuary takes up more than half the island's land mass and is home to a wide variety of bird life. I am always keen to photograph the roseate spoonbills with their splendid pink feathers when they are close to shore at low tide.

A small bridge connects Sanibel to charming Captiva Island, where the mouthwatering Key lime pie at the Keylime Bistro lures us in before we take a charter boat ride to secluded North Captiva Island or Cayo Costa State Park, an area full of pristine and nearly deserted beaches. The former fishing grounds of the Calusa Tribe, Cayo Costa has 9 miles of undeveloped shoreline for swimming, snorkeling,

Points of INTEREST

REST STOPS

If your Florida itinerary includes a visit to Captiva Island, a slice of sweet-tart Key lime pie from Keylime Bistro is a must. *keylimebistro captiva.com*

You'll find myriad restaurants serving up rib-sticking Caribbean cuisine in Key West's Bahama Village. *keywestchamber.org*

NOT TO BE MISSED

Cruising Everglades National Park aboard an airboat is the best way to see the area's unique landscape. There are three authorized tour companies in the park: Coopertown Airboats, Everglades Safari Park and Gator Park. They are all located along U.S. Highway 41/ the Tamiami Trail. *nps.gov/ever*

WORDS TO THE WISE

If you happen to be in The Key West Butterfly and Nature Conservancy between 4:45 and 5:45 p.m., you can reserve a spot to "flamingle" with Scarlett and Rhett, the resident flamingos. *keywestbutterfly.com*

▼

A butterfly feeds at the Key West Butterfly and Nature Conservancy.

shelling, fishing and birding. The best part is that the island is only accessible by kayak or boat, so there are fewer visitors, making for a pleasant and relaxed atmosphere.

Our trip in the Everglades starts on a section of the Tamiami Trail, or U.S. Highway 41, as it makes its way through Big Cypress National Preserve. This is where the famed Everglades experience really begins for us.

Travel along the Tamiami is slower going than along Interstate 75 (known as Alligator Alley) to the north, but the unhurried pace allows for plenty of relaxed stops at inspiring places, such as famed black-and-white photographer Clyde Butcher's gallery in the town of Ochopee. Butcher was instrumental in saving the area's diverse ecosystems from development.

To see the interior of the Everglades, climb aboard an airboat and allow it to whisk you away into the expanse. You'll find plenty of local tour companies to choose from along the highway. When the boats slow down in the saw-grass channels, it is an ideal opportunity to see Florida's most famous native

resident: the alligator. I always marvel at how Native Americans and early European explorers got their bearings in this flat, featureless and seemingly endless horizon.

Back on the Tamiami, we often take a side trip on the 27-mile Loop Road through Big Cypress National Preserve. This gravel road leads to some amazing wildlife viewing. We frequently stop to gaze into the cypress swamp and are rewarded with sightings of alligators, birds and turtles. I'm especially awed by how the beautiful white plumage of snowy and great egrets contrasts with the showy red blooms of cardinal air plants, or bromeliads, hanging from bald cypress trees.

And we love stopping at small towns along the way, including Everglades City, where you can gaze out onto one of the islands of Ten Thousand Islands National Wildlife Refuge while enjoying ultrafresh seafood; a cold drink; and my favorite, crab cakes.

Nature abounds here in refuges such as Fakahatchee Strand Preserve State Park (Florida's largest state park) and Corkscrew Swamp Sanctuary. When we revisit our favorite places, we always find something new. Spotting the tiny burrowing owls at Marco Island and Cape Coral is high on my wish list for our upcoming trip.

Using the city of Homestead as our base, we head into Everglades National Park, home to the largest subtropical wilderness in the United States. Here, a slow-moving river flows through a seemingly endless flat prairie of saw grass, interrupted only by occasional hammocks (stands of trees on slightly higher ground). I cherish visiting the park at sunrise, when it is alive with the sounds of endless bird chatter. A closer inspection reveals incredible views of numerous bird species wading and feeding in the shallow waters. This national park is a birders paradise. While strolling along the boardwalk at the Pa-hay-okee Overlook one morning, my wife and I saw a family of barred owls at close range. A fledgling was near while the mother kept a close look and the father hunted in the saw grass. We savored this encounter with nature.

Our journey continues on one of my absolute favorite drives: Highway 1. This route connects the enchantingly narrow strip of islands forming the Florida Keys.

This mostly deserted chain separates the Atlantic Ocean to the east and the Gulf of Mexico to the northwest. We pass through tiny towns blessed with small seafood restaurants, colorful buildings and panoramic views on both sides of the highway. The road leads to a stunning landscape ringed by the sea, full of wildlife both on land and below the water.

Some species of plants and animals are found only here, such as the tiny Key deer, an endangered white-tailed deer subspecies that stands 3 feet tall, and the largest coral reef ecosystem in the continental United States. In fact, there are four wildlife refuges in the Keys, including the National Key Deer

Look for this selfie-worthy sign at the historic Key West Bight Marina.

An airboat glides through waters too shallow for regular boats in Everglades National Park.

Refuge. John Pennekamp Coral Reef State Park in Key Largo was the first underwater preserve to be established in the United States.

Bahia Honda State Park in Big Pine Key is another natural treasure with fantastic beach views. In addition to one of America's largest remaining stands of silver palm trees, you will find the Bahia Honda Bridge, a historic remnant of Henry Flagler's railroad, which was the first mode of transportation through the Keys. History is everywhere.

Be sure to take some time to relax on the park's lovely beaches. Try sitting under the shade of a resident palm tree with a book about the Keys or a novel by one-time resident Ernest Hemingway. The repetition of waves crashing onto the shoreline serves as a near-hypnotic soundtrack for reading in solitude.

Our final destination is the storied town of Key West, where restaurants and tourist shops are plentiful. We tend to prefer what the quieter side of town,

Bahama Village, has to offer. Colorful gypsy chickens wander about on quaint streets that are ideal for a stroll. And Fort Zachary Taylor State Park is a must-see for military history buffs. The red-brick structure has the largest collection of Civil War armaments in the world, and the fort itself played an important role in that war and the Spanish-American War.

If it is sunny, we rent cruiser bikes and ride a loop through this historic part of town and along the beach. If the weather turns, we head to the Key West Butterfly and Nature Conservancy, to admire the exotic plants and vibrant, fluttering butterflies.

Watching a tropical sunset in Key West at the southernmost point in the continental United States is a must. To watch the sunset from the water, book an evening cruise on a schooner. This really caps a wonderful day in Florida. If you're anything like me, you might just fly back here next year. ●

STORY BY
ANDREA CAUGHEY

SAVANNAH

FROM CHARMING SHOPS TO COBBLESTONE PLAZAS, THIS HISTORIC CITY BRIMS WITH SOUTHERN FLAIR.

WITH ITS MOSS-LADEN gardens, historic architecture and down-home cuisine, Savannah is an idyllic destination for a weekend getaway.

I was able to tour virtually all of Savannah's historic district by foot, but trolleys, bikes, carriages and buses are other options to tour the city's churches and graveyards, forts, inns, pocket gardens and museums.

I reveled in Savannah's artistic side, browsing creative boutiques such as Paris Market & Brocante, a treasure trove of eclectic finds in a Victorian grocery store, and ShopSCAD, the gallery store for the nearby Savannah College of Art and Design.

After lots of walking and shopping, comfort food was a must, so I stopped in for a delicious meal at Mrs. Wilkes' Dining Room, a beloved lunch spot with hearty southern favorites.

My idyllic weekend culminated in a stroll along River Street. Vintage buildings and warehouses along the water drew me in with a tantalizing blend of arts and crafts, antiques, sweet treats and Southern charm. ▪

▾
Forsyth Park's elegant fountain anchors the historic district.

Horses race to the finish line in this stirring installation at Thoroughbred Park.

STORY BY
KATHY WITT

HORSE COUNTRY

THE SOUND OF HOOFBEATS SPURS KATHY WITT THROUGH CENTRAL KENTUCKY.

THE CHARMING RETIREE on the other side of the fence keeps kissing and nuzzling my hand. I remark on how handsome he is. Then I offer him a carrot.

I'm in Kentucky horse country, at the Old Friends Thoroughbred Retirement Farm, visiting some equine residents. More than 100 horses—including 1997 Kentucky Derby and Preakness champ Silver Charm—are living the good life here. Even Popcorn Deelites, the star of the movie *Seabiscuit,* called this place home for a while.

My husband, John, and I are Sunday-driving back roads framed by stands of trees turning orange, red and russet as fall sweeps through central Kentucky.

Old Friends, in Georgetown, is our first stop. Georgetown is also known as "Kentucky horse headquarters" for its abundance of horsey attractions. A few of these include stables, festivals and the equestrian-themed art galleries of painter Robert Clark and photographer

John Stephen Hockensmith. Visitors will discover even more local treasures inside the boutiques and restaurants that line downtown Georgetown's Victorian streetscape.

Kentucky horse country stretches all the way from Lexington to Shelbyville to Oldham County and beyond. On our way from Georgetown to Lexington, the "horse capital of the world," we drive along winding country roads lined with miles of black paddock fencing as well as historic dry-stone fences. Driving by Thoroughbred Park, with its bronze racehorses poised hoofbeats away from the finish line, really sets the tone.

Our next stop is the Kentucky Horse Park. Picturesque grounds with lush foliage, trim white barns and stables paint a fitting backdrop for monuments to these majestic animals, including a life-size sculpture of Man o' War—one of the greatest racehorses ever—rising nobly from his perch.

Points of INTEREST

REST STOP

If you're looking for the royal treatment, book a stay at Georgetown's B&B at Queenslake. This stunning residence sits on sprawling grounds that boast a lake, rolling pastures and an enchanted forest. The accommodating innkeeper even likes to grant requests with the response, "As you wish." *queenslake.com*

NEARBY ATTRACTIONS

In Georgetown, step through the Tokugawa gate to enter Yuko-En on the Elkhorn, the four-season Kentucky-Japan Friendship Garden. The Japanese-style strolling garden offers visitors a peaceful oasis of color and fragrance, waterfalls, a koi pond and a traditional Japanese rock garden. *yukoen.com*

Hermitage Farm, in Oldham County, offers organic farm-to-table dinners and picnic lunches, tours of the grounds and the chance to learn about carriages used in the 1939 classic *Gone with the Wind*. *hermitagefarm.com*

▼

Politician Henry Clay lived at Ashland on the outskirts of Lexington.

John and I then make our way to the park's International Museum of the Horse. We first zoom through millions of years of horse history in the Legacy of the Horse exhibit, then slow things down at the Al-Marah Horse Galleries and its Black Stallion Experience to see the movie clips, books and other interactive exhibits that feature the Arabian horse of literature and film.

Our heads swimming with newfound knowledge, we leave the Black Stallion Experience and head to the George Ford Morris Gallery at the American Saddlebred Museum nearby, where we see this painter's love of the breed portrayed through his art. We admire portraits of some of the early 20th century's most celebrated horses—Roxie Highland, Beau Peavine and American Born.

A 20-minute drive south from the museum brings us to the Henry Clay estate at Ashland, where a statue of a thoroughbred sipping water welcomes us. The estate feels like a secret garden, its iron gates opening to a traditional English parterre garden, hundreds of old-growth trees, walking trails and centuries-old outbuildings. The 17-acre estate was once home to the American statesman and orator, who was also one of the most respected horse breeders and scientific farmers of his time.

Heading west from this "capital," we arrive at another—Shelbyville County, the "American saddlebred capital of the world." Here, even more paddocks stretch across gently undulating hills as we roll through the countryside. The sight of the horses frisking along the fence line never gets old.

A scenic tour of Kismet Farm is our chance to see American saddlebreds, high-stepping show horses known for their grace and athleticism. We make a quick stop at Shelby Horse Supply to browse among the tack (bridles, reins and halters) in a shop known for its handcrafted leather goods. Our mission is to find a souvenir that captures the spirit of our journey through Kentucky horse country. We find it in the form of a chestnut leather keychain with an engravable plate.

Because writing children's books has always been a dream of mine, a visit to LaGrange's Windy Meadows Horse Farm is a must. Not only can you learn about horses of all breeds on a guided tour, you'll also get to meet owner Ellie Troutman, author of the charmingly illustrated children's book *The Tails of Windy Meadows*. The book details a day in the life of a Kentucky horse farm as told through its barn dwellers. Movie buffs will enjoy learning that several Hallmark movies, including 2016's *The Ultimate Legacy*, were filmed here, and you'll have the chance to see some film locations, props and costume pieces on the tour.

Though I'm a native Kentuckian, I wasn't lucky enough to grow up around horses. Watching them gallop across fields, nicker in the pasture and eat carrots from my hand always feels like a treat—even more so when the pretty-as-a-picture scenery has been brushed with autumn's colorful palette. ◗

▼
Say "hay" to the local residents!

▼

The Cane River, which is actually an oxbow lake, is the heart of downtown Natchitoches.

STORY BY
MAGGIE HEYN RICHARDSON

CANE RIVER

DISCOVER LOUISIANA'S CREOLE CROSSROADS ALONG THE
CANE RIVER NATIONAL HERITAGE TRAIL.

YOU COULD MAKE a strong argument that live oaks are the world's most beautiful trees. Their moss-draped limbs reach wide and high, transforming the open Louisiana landscape into something at once elegant and haunting. On the Cane River National Heritage Trail in the northern part of the state, live oaks punctuate a meandering trip along a winding river through fertile farmland and gentle hills. The Bayou State is chock-full of history, and here some of its most interesting stories uncoil.

Established in 1994, the trail follows the approximately 35-mile route of the Cane River, which is actually a narrow oxbow lake. The town of Natchitoches (locals pronounce it NACK-a-dish), which consistently ranks as one of the county's most charming small towns, is the trail's centerpiece. Extending west and south, the route reveals 300 years of history, capturing natural splendor and cultural complexity along the way.

I start my exploration of the Cane River Trail in Natchitoches. Founded in 1714 by French settlers who were eager to trade with the nearby Caddo Native

Americans, Natchitoches is Louisiana's oldest permanent European settlement, older even than New Orleans, which was established four years later.

On Jefferson Street overlooking the Cane River waterfront, I get acquainted with the past at Fort St. Jean Baptiste State Historic Site, where a replica fort and trading post show how French settlers lived. From the visitors center, I make my way outside along a shady path where cabins, a cooking hearth, a church, a mercantile and more bring back 18th-century life.

The French weren't the only ones to settle these parts. The eastern edge of what was once New Spain lies about 14 miles from here. I drive west along Highway 6 to Los Adaes State Historic Site, once a Spanish presidio, or fort, and the former capital of Spain's Texas territory. Highway 6 actually marks the overland route used by the Spanish, El Camino Real ("the royal road"). Los Adaes, a lush outdoor site, once held a hexagonal Spanish fort. It has yielded a trove of archaeological finds over the years and is a perfect place to stretch

Points of INTEREST

NOT TO BE MISSED
Stroll or relax in a horse-drawn carriage as you take in the sites and shops in Natchitoches' 33-block National Historic Landmark District. The area is known for its diverse architecture; you'll spot Victorian, Art Deco, Queen Anne, Federal and Spanish Revival influences as you make your way from building to building.

FUN FACT
Robert Harling wrote his stage play *Steel Magnolias* in Natchitoches, and the movie adaption was also was filmed in town. Folksy tours bring you to locations where memorable scenes took place. *natchitoches.com*

SIDE TRIP
An easy daytrip from Natchitoches, the Kisatchie National Forest covers more than 600,000 acres of recreational land. Enjoy stunning hikes through longleaf pine forests as well as birding, camping, fishing and other outdoor activities. *fs.usda.gov/kisatchie*

▼
This cabin at Oakland Plantation once served as slave quarters.

my legs, read about life for the soldiers here and listen to the rhythmic cackle of a nearby pileated woodpecker.

Next, I head back to Natchitoches to explore its downtown. Awash in Creole and Art Deco architecture, the area includes a 33-block National Historic Landmark District you can enjoy on foot or by horse-drawn carriage. The Cane River waterfront is also great for strolling, and decorative park benches under magnolia trees offer views of the river. Kayakers are enjoying the water today, their paddles slicing through the placid, glassy surface as the sun beams down from above.

I stroll along Front Street, admiring the numerous wrought iron-trimmed storefronts. One shop that has been frequently recommended to me is the Kaffie-Frederick General Mercantile,

a two-story emporium founded in 1863. Downstairs, I find shelves packed with tools, hardware and gifts, while the upstairs holds trendy housewares. My favorite part of shopping here is paying for my purchases (some vintage toys and cheeky cocktail napkins) at the 1910 cash register.

I'm starting to get hungry, so I head around the corner to Lasyone's Meat Pie Kitchen on 2nd Street. The cafe has served the community's signature dish since 1967. Meat pies are a tradition in Natchitoches—there's even a fall meat pie festival complete with cook-offs, live music and the crowning of the Miss Natchitoches Meat Pie Queen. I order a couple of meat pies to go and set out to explore the downriver portion of the heritage trail, where Louisiana's rich Creole history comes alive in the land.

Swamps and wetlands may be the typical Louisiana landscape, but here you see swaths of farmland and groves of massive hardwoods. Ten miles south of Natchitoches along quiet Highway 494 lies the Cane River Creole National Historical Park. The site is run by the National Park Service and includes the two most intact French Creole cotton plantations in the country: Oakland and Magnolia. At Oakland, 16 historic buildings—including the main house, slave or tenant farmer quarters and a general store—paint a picture of how enslaved people once lived here. This portion of the Cane River Trail also includes Isle Brevelle, where the Creole descendants of enslaved Africans and French planters lived as free people of color.

Five miles farther downriver, I reach Melrose Plantation. Touring Melrose, I learn about one of the American folk art world's great stories. The plantation became an artists colony in the early 20th century, and on a chance occasion, a visiting artist left behind his supplies. A cook who worked at Melrose named Clementine Hunter picked them up and began using them, soon discovering that she had both passion and talent. Clementine's folk paintings eventually earned attention and international acclaim. I head to the second floor of the African House building to see her stunning murals of Cane River life.

I end the day by watching the sunset at St. Augustine Catholic Church and Cemetery, established in the early 19th century by and for local Creoles at a lovely bend in the river. The church is still operational today and is also a part of Louisiana's African American Heritage Trail. I stroll the peaceful grounds and gravesites.

As I walk through the sanctuary, the day's last rays of sunlight play through stained-glass windows. It's a fine place to reflect on the area's history, beauty and resilience. ❧

JONATHAN NUTT/GETTY IMAGES

▼
The Kisatchie National Forest is an easy daytrip from Natchitoches.

The Monocacy River aqueduct is the largest and most impressive of those built along the C&O canal.

STORY AND PHOTOS BY
PAT & CHUCK BLACKLEY

CHESAPEAKE & OHIO CANAL

HIKE, BIKE OR FLOAT ALONG THIS MARYLAND CANAL FOR A TRIP BACK IN TIME.

WE FIRST DISCOVERED the Chesapeake & Ohio Canal many years ago on a trip to Harpers Ferry National Historical Park in West Virginia. When we saw some folks walking across the Potomac River into Maryland via a converted railroad bridge, we followed suit and found ourselves on a lovely scenic trail.

Along the way, we were drawn to the historic lift locks, lockhouses and other old canal remnants. After returning home, we began researching the canal and set out to visit all the interesting places along its nearly 185 miles.

Visitors can start in the middle of the bustling Georgetown neighborhood in Washington, D.C., and hike, bike or cross-country ski to reach Cumberland, Maryland, on the Allegheny Plateau.

The level, traffic-free route passes through beautiful countryside without crossing any busy roads, a rarity in the highly developed eastern United States.

Waterways and canals like this one were crucial to America's prosperity before railroads were introduced. More than 3,000 miles of canals were built between the late 1700s and mid-1800s to transport goods inland from the coast.

Merchants were eager for a waterway that would connect the coastline with the resources of the Ohio River Valley, and they saw the Potomac River as the most logical route.

But perilous waterfalls and rapids were serious obstacles. Eventually, the C&O Co. made plans for a canal that would run parallel to the river.

On July 4, 1828, work began at Little Falls, Maryland. Due to labor problems and huge engineering challenges, the construction of the canal cost more than $11 million and lasted 22 years.

The first section opened as early as 1830, with the last section opening in 1850 when the C&O Canal came to a halt in Cumberland, well short of its original destination near Pittsburgh.

The canal nevertheless operated for nearly a century. At its peak, up to

Points of INTEREST

REST STOP
Seven historic lockhouses along the route of the canal are available to rent for overnight stays. Each lockhouse sleeps eight guests and is outfitted with historically inspired furnishings. Linens are not provided, so be sure to bring your own. For more information about the amenities in each lockhouse, visit *canaltrust.org /programs/canal -quarters*.

NEARBY ATTRACTION
Canal Place, in Cumberland, commemorates the C&O Canal's western terminus and has also been designated as Maryland's first certified heritage area. Throughout the summer, visitors can participate in a variety of activities, including canal boat replica tours, scenic rail excursions, and festivals. It's also a welcome boon for hikers, cyclists and joggers. *passagesofthe potomac.org*

▼

At Great Falls Tavern, guides lead mules pulling reproduction boats.

850,000 tons of material, such as coal and lumber, moved through the canal per year. As many as 500 boats ran simultaneously, pulled by mules that walked alongside on a towpath.

Railroads were a big contributor to the canal's obsolescence, and after a particularly damaging flood in 1924, the canal closed, ending a way of life for many boat captains and lockkeepers (who lived in the lockhouses with their families). The canal was purchased by the federal government in 1938 and placed under control of the National Park Service. It was designated as a National Historical Park in 1971.

Along the route, there are several access points and visitors centers with helpful maps and information to guide you on your journey. You can spend the night under the stars at a campground or even stay in a restored lockhouse.

Over the years, we've visited most of the canal's major features. The large Paw Paw Tunnel on the West Virginia-Maryland border is one of our favorites, especially for Chuck, a civil engineer.

Built to bypass a 6-mile stretch of river at the Paw Paw Bends, it runs for 3,118 feet below a mountain. A walk through it is a real adventure, but be sure to take along a flashlight, because it's eerily dark inside.

In Potomac, Maryland, the canal shares the limelight with the Great Falls of the Potomac. Here, the mighty river plunges dramatically over a series of jagged rocks and rushes through Mather Gorge, creating an absolutely awe-inspiring sight.

A visitors center is located in the Great Falls Tavern, which was added on to the original lockhouse in 1831. From spring through fall, you can ride on a reproduction canal boat towed by mules. And for history buffs like us, a large number of original operational structures can be found in and around Williamsport, Maryland.

The C&O Canal was very ambitious for its time and is truly an engineering marvel. We're lucky to have this piece of American transportation history preserved for our enjoyment. ●

STORY AND PHOTOS BY
SYLVIA PURVIS

NESHOBA COUNTY FAIR

THIS EIGHT-DAY FESTIVAL OFFERS GUESTS A CENTURY'S WORTH OF CELEBRATION.

FOR MORE THAN 125 years, Mississippi's Giant House Party has taken place in Philadelphia, Mississippi. Known as the Neshoba County Fair, it began in 1889 as an agricultural picnic for farmers and their wives to show off livestock, crops and handiwork. After two years, the event was organized as the Stock and Agricultural Fair, with a board of directors and officers.

Thousands of brave souls travel across the county, state and nation every July to spend up to eight days baking in the sweltering Mississippi heat and to bunk up in the cramped confines of a cabin.

Family tradition is big at the fair. Cabins are prime real estate and are often passed down from generation to generation. It's as if a little town gets populated overnight.

There are about 600 cabins on the property and more than 575 RV spots with a waiting list. All of the cabins now have power and running water. The exteriors are often painted with garish colors, so they stand out from their neighbors. Some are painted in

Fairgoers flock to their cabins for horse racing, music and more.

Points of INTEREST

REST STOP

Several motels are available in the area, and there is RV parking at the fairgrounds. For more information about lodging, visit *neshobacounty fair.org*.

SIDE TRIP

Rowan Oak, in Oxford, was the home of American author William Faulkner. The stately antebellum house and lush grounds are available for tours. *rowanoak.com*

NEARBY ATTRACTION

The Jimmie Rodgers Museum, in Meridian, celebrates the life and career of "the father of country music." The building resembles a train station, complete with an engine and caboose outside, in a nod to Rodgers' other moniker, "the singing brakeman." Original recordings and sheet music for Rodgers' songs, as well as his denim jacket and other belongings, are displayed here, and in the spring Meridian sponsors a Jimmie Rodgers Memorial Festival. *jimmierodgers.com*

▼

A historic marker drives home the fairground's cultural significance.

honor of favorite college teams. The cabin owners are generally very friendly and happy to share a spot on the porch or a cold glass of sweet tea or lemonade with visitors.

Founder's Square is the scene of lively political speeches. National, local, district and state candidates and elected officials have spoken at the pavilion since 1896. Presidential candidate Ronald Reagan spoke in 1980, John Glenn visited in 1983 and Michael Dukakis attended in 1988.

Throughout the Neshoba County Fair's eight-day run, traditions are upheld. The fair always begins on a Friday and ends the following Friday during the last week of July. As with the first fair, agricultural crops, 4-H exhibits and crafts are on display in the Exhibit Hall.

The festivities on that first Friday night include a calf scramble that is followed by the Smith, Harper &

Morgan PRCA Rodeo. Later that evening, a festive mood takes over as dancing and live music begin on Founder's Square.

Saturday starts with an arts and crafts market and a triathlon. A mule pull is held at the grandstand in the afternoon. Another rodeo takes place in the evening, followed by more music and dancing.

On Sunday morning, a worship service is held on Founder's Square. After lunch, the grandstand fills with fans of mule and horse races, which run each afternoon for the remainder of the week. Other events include a youth talent show, a cakewalk, an antique car show, a beauty pageant, concerts and more.

The midway and concession area opens each day at 1 p.m. There, you'll find a merry-go-round, Ferris wheel and entertaining side booths. The whole week is like one big party. ●

STORY BY
JENNY WISNIEWSKI

FLAT ROCK

FROM HISTORIC SITES TO HIKING TRAILS TO MOVIE-SET MOUNTAIN VIEWS, FLAT ROCK, NORTH CAROLINA, IS PURE POETRY.

BLESSED WITH fragrant orchards, lush forests and intriguing historic sites nearby, Flat Rock, North Carolina, personifies quaint charm. Its backdrop of gorgeous scenery and activities for all ages make this quiet community an alluring weekend getaway that invites you to slow down, enjoy nature and learn something new.

My memories of Flat Rock exist as a series of stored images over the course of 20 years. When my parents moved to Flat Rock after retiring, there was just a post office, a gift shop and a deli attached to a gas station. A few other businesses have cropped up since then, but the town remains sleepy, and that's just the way residents like it.

This one-traffic-light town was settled first by Cherokee Indians and later by coastal South Carolinians who built homes in the mountains to escape the summertime heat and humidity. One of the earliest of these wayfarers, Charles

▼
Poet Carl Sandburg was inspired by this natural paradise.

Points of INTEREST

REST STOPS

The aroma alone will draw you in to Hubba Hubba Smokehouse. This barbecue joint slow-cooks its pork and beef brisket in a wood-fired pit. Be sure to order southern sides like succotash, pimiento cheese grits and Henderson County apple slaw. *hubba hubbasmokehouse .squarespace.com*

You could not find a more lovely setting than Highland Lake Inn & Resort. The 26-acre resort offers a swimming pool and complimentary bikes, canoes, kayaks and paddleboats. Accommodations include rustic cabins, a historic inn and poolside cottages. *hliresort.com*

NOT TO BE MISSED

The 100-acre Sky Top Orchard, which boasts 25 varieties of apples, is a must-see during an autumn getaway. Take in the mountain views while enjoying a hayride. Pick your own apples or visit the pumpkin patch. Be sure to taste the famous apple cider doughnuts fresh from the fryer. *skytoporchard.com*

▼

Visitors can feed the animals in the barn at Connemara.

Baring of the English Baring brothers banking family, discovered Flat Rock in 1827, created his own 400-acre country estate and then sold property to other Charlestonians. Flat Rock came to be known as the "little Charleston of the mountains." Some of those homes still stand today, and Flat Rock is now listed on the National Register of Historic Places.

One of the most popular National Historic Sites, Connemara, was the beloved home of poet and biographer Carl Sandburg's family for 22 years. He and his wife, Lilian, arrived in 1945 with their three daughters, two grandchildren and 16,000 volumes of books. Their large but unassuming home perches on a hill overlooking a placid pond, with Big Glassy Mountain,

the highest point in the area, looming in the distance. The main house has been preserved as the Sandburgs left it, the poet's guitar propped on a chair, his library intact.

A tour guide in the Sandburg house once explained to me the rhythm of the Sandburgs' lives here at this 240-acre parcel of paradise in the mountains. Carl Sandburg's creative hours started around dusk. In the wee hours of the morning, he and his wife would then pass each other like ships in the night as he headed to bed and she began her day, caring for her goats.

We visited the goat barn and learned all about the breeding work begun by Lilian. My kids delighted in venturing through the pasture, feed slipping through their fingers as Chikaming goats surrounded them, knowing a snack was at hand.

Across the street from Connemara sits another iconic spot, the Flat Rock Playhouse. Opened in 1952 and proudly designated the State Theatre of North Carolina, it stages comedies, dramas, youth theater, concerts and Broadway musicals for eight months of the year. With its rustic red barn-like exterior, it blends right into the small-town country setting.

Kitty-corner from the playhouse, several brightly painted shops called Little Rainbow Row beckon browsers. The anchor, The Wrinkled Egg, was built in 1891 and originally housed the town's general store. Behind the shops sits a courtyard with picnic tables and magnolia trees, where townsfolk and visitors gather. After an afternoon of hiking, nothing beats enjoying pizza or barbecue, sharing conversation and savoring the slowness of small-town southern life.

A few years before my first tour of Connemara, I visited what was then the 10,000-acre DuPont property, only 13 miles from Flat Rock. Back then, only organized hiking clubs were invited onto the private property, and fortunately my parents belonged to one.

On the day of my DuPont visit, we hiked 6 miles round trip to Bridal Veil Falls, where water spills off an overhanging ledge, forming a vertical plane that crashes into the pool below. Its deafening roar and misty spray are all-immersive (probably the reason it was selected for a scene in the movie *The Last of the Mohicans*).

Featuring five impressive waterfalls, the DuPont property was once a bit of a mystery to most. I was pleased to learn that since my initial visit, it had been designated a State Recreational Forest and was now open to the public. In addition to great hiking and biking trails, the park holds five lakes and nearly 18 miles of trout streams.

▼

DuPont State Recreational Forest's Triple Falls shimmers in the sun.

▼

A short hike from the Blue Ridge Flat Rock overlook reveals a vista full of autumn color.

The last time I visited Flat Rock, the trail leading to the top of Big Glassy Mountain was practically calling my name. With my infant son strapped to my back, my older son running ahead and my dad at my side, we climbed the familiar trail. The hike is short enough for young feet—under 3 miles round trip—and the breathtaking prize at the top is well worth the effort. Standing on a large outcropping of sloped rock, we gazed out at an autumnal dreamscape of scarlet dogwood, saffron hickory and bright orange sassafras sprawling out in front of us.

From this vantage point, it was as if all civilization had faded away. Soon my dad would stare at a different beauty— the pristine, monochromatic austerity of winter—and I would be swallowed back into bustling civilization. But I would carry with me fond memories of crisp, clear mountain air, small-town friendliness and precious time spent with family in the quiet, natural beauty of Flat Rock. ◗

STORY BY
PAULETTE M. ROY

HUNTING ISLAND

ON THIS UNDEVELOPED ISLAND, THE FORESTS WADE IN THE OCEAN AND THE MARSHES ARE FULL OF LIFE.

HUNTING ISLAND STATE PARK always beckons us to sneak a detour into our annual drive from Massachusetts to Florida. Just north of Savannah, Georgia, along the Atlantic Coast, this 5,000-acre park is one of only a few undeveloped sea islands in this region. There's never enough time to photograph its sandy beaches, extensive saltwater marshes and dense maritime forests of slash pine, palmetto and live oak.

Because it buffers the inland South Carolina coast from the wild Atlantic, Hunting Island continually transforms under forces of erosion. At sunrise, we often explore the beach, photographing a coastal landscape that looks entirely different than it did on our last visit. We point our cameras toward dunes that shift and forests with ocean-wave floors. Once the sun kisses the horizon, we turn our backs to it and capture the warm gold highlights glinting off the historic lighthouse.

The original lighthouse, constructed in the 1850s, was destroyed during a Civil War battle. In 1875, the current structure was built of cast-iron sections designed to be dismantled so it could

▼

The island's historic lighthouse stands 136 feet tall.

PAUL REZENDES

Points of INTEREST

REST STOP
Hunting Island has one cabin that can be reserved for stays of 2 days or more. The cabin, which has a charming screened porch, is equipped with many modern conveniences and located quite close to the lighthouse. Visitors can also stay the night at a nearby campground.

WORDS TO THE WISE
Venture out to Paradise Pier, which is at the southern end of the island, and chances are you'll find a good spot to spy dolphins.

NEARBY ATTRACTION
Neighboring Saint Helena Island is home to the Penn Center, an African American cultural center that preserves and honors the history of the Gullah Geechee people. It's located on the campus of the former Penn School, one of the nation's first schools founded to educate African American students. *penncenter.com*

▼
Wind and water shape Hunting Island's sandy dunes and shoreline.

move. And yes, only 14 years later, Hunting Island's shrinking shoreline created such a need. The lighthouse was relocated a little more than a mile inland to its present location. Climbing the 167 steps to the observation deck rewards visitors with a panoramic view of the Atlantic Ocean and the island's coastal scenery.

Along Sea Island Parkway, or U.S. Highway 21, we find many convenient places to pull off the road for wildlife viewing. Stop by stop, we make our way to Hunting Island's south end, where a nature center spotlights live animals, an aquarium and natural history exhibits. If you're still looking for

something to do, borrow a rod and reel from the center—no charge—and try your luck angling from the adjacent pier. Or access one of the hiking and biking trails that snake northward along the saltwater lagoon. Either way, the bird-watching is superb.

As the afternoon wanes, we walk to the salt marsh and hike out on the boardwalk. Below, hundreds of fiddler crabs scurry to and from their holes, entertaining us with their jittery antics. After taking a minute to admire our surroundings, we set up the camera on the dock, about a half-mile out, and wait for the sun to bring a vibrant grand finale to another perfect trip. ◗

STORY BY
MARIJA ANDRIC

Tennessee

COCKE COUNTY

THIS WELL-ROUNDED REGION WELCOMES NATURE LOVERS AND ADVENTURE SEEKERS OF ALL STRIPES.

WITH THREE RIVERS (Pigeon, French Broad and Nolichucky), a national park (Great Smoky Mountains), a national forest (Cherokee) and a state forest (Martha Sundquist), Cocke County, Tennessee, is a paradise for outdoorsy types.

Rafting is big here, with most of the action taking place on the white water of the upper Pigeon River. If you'd like a smoother ride, a calmer route awaits you on the lower Pigeon River.

Horseback riding is another favorite pastime. At the secluded French Broad River Outpost Ranch, which sits on 346 acres in the Smoky Mountains, visitors can choose from five riding trails. The ranch also gives families a rare chance to step away from technology—there are no TVs in the rooms, and cellphones won't work here.

Rankin Bottoms offers excellent birding throughout the year. Great blue herons and double-crested cormorants can be spotted in the summer and fall. In winter, ducks and geese take to the waters, and in spring, large numbers of songbirds let their melodies soar.

By water or by land, on the back of a horse or behind binoculars, there's so much natural beauty to explore in Cocke County, Tennessee. ✸

▼

Water flows to fun in the Smokies.

STORY AND PHOTOS BY
SUSAN TERRY

CHINCOTEAGUE

THIS VIRGINIA ISLAND AND THE WILD PONIES ACROSS THE
WATER LIVE UP TO A YOUNG GIRL'S DREAMS.

GROWING UP in the 1950s as a horse-crazy young girl, I read the book *Misty of Chincoteague* by Marguerite Henry. I imagined myself on Chincoteague Island off the coast of Virginia with the Beebe kids and the beautiful ponies— never thinking I would actually travel there. Fast-forward to June 2018, and I found myself on the island with my husband, Lloyd, as we celebrated our 50th wedding anniversary.

Chincoteague and Assateague Islands are side-by-side natural treasures in the Atlantic Ocean. The islands are home to the Chincoteague National Wildlife Refuge and the Assateague Island National Seashore. While cars are allowed on the islands, the speed limit is 25 mph, and we never saw any speeders!

We stayed at The Watson Guest House on Chincoteague, and we had the whole place to ourselves. Our kind innkeeper, Annette, made us feel right at home and served a hearty and delicious breakfast each morning. We enjoyed eating out on the porch in the beautiful weather.

A highlight of our time on the island, of course, was boarding the boat from Daisey's Island Cruises for a floating journey to Assateague, where the wild ponies live. Our helpful guide, Alex, took us directly to several spots where they graze.

Alex, an area local, helps with Pony Penning week every July. After being rounded up, the wild ponies swim across the channel at a time between tides when the current is low. Many of the young foals are auctioned off (some as "buybacks" that rejoin the island's wild herds), with proceeds supporting the local volunteer fire department— a tradition that has helped control the herds since 1925. The rest of the ponies then swim back across the channel.

There are opportunities to see ponies even if you aren't one for boat rides. I saw a number of domesticated ponies grazing contentedly in a corral next to the McDonald's on Chincoteague.

Back on the shore, we relaxed and took in the ocean view. Listening to the waves, seeing the sparkle of sunlit diamonds on the water and checking the sand for shells made for a very peaceful morning.

The trip was truly a dream vacation for me. I felt the spirit of Misty taking me back to a time long ago when I, too, could fly like the wind on the back of my very own wild pony. ●

Top: Wild ponies graze on grass along Assateague Island. Bottom: Island Creamery has been serving up homemade ice cream made from local fruits and dairy for 46 years. This family-owned shop is an island institution.

TOP: VW PICS/GETTY IMAGES; BOTTOM: KELLY CONKIN

Points of INTEREST

REST STOP
Dig in to a crabcake at Don's Seafood Restaurant, which has been serving fresh-caught fare since 1973. *donsseafood restaurant.com*

NOT TO BE MISSED
A storehouse of historical island treasures, the fascinating Museum of Chincoteague Island celebrates the people, culture and heritage of the island. Visitors can participate in scavenger hunts for all ages or visit an exhibit featuring the real Misty pony. *chincoteague museum.com*

At Flying Fish Gallery, you'll discover unique works from local artists who often use castoff materials. Handmade jewelry, suncatchers and garden wind spinners handcrafted out of tablespoons make great souvenirs. *flyingfishci.com*

FUN FACT
Chincoteague was named after a Native American word meaning "beautiful land across the water."

▼
Stunning views reward hikers on the Endless Wall Trail in New River Gorge National Park and Preserve.

STORY BY
JILL GLEESON

NEW RIVER GORGE

JILL GLEESON EXPLORES THE RUSHING WATERS AND FIERY FOLIAGE OF AMERICA'S NEWEST NATIONAL PARK.

IT'S A PERFECT AFTERNOON in West Virginia. Sunny, with bright blue skies and temperatures in the 70s, it's the kind of weather the mid-Atlantic region is famous for in autumn. By all accounts, Long Point Trail should be bustling with hikers and mountain bikers. It's known to be one of the most popular paths in West Virginia's New River Gorge National Park and Preserve, the country's most recent national park.

The designation, which took effect in 2021, is an upgrade of sorts from the national river status the New River Gorge earned in 1978. And it's already brought more adventure seekers into the official boundaries of the gorge area. For park service purposes, those confines run for 53 wild miles from the town of Hinton north to Hawks Nest and encompass 70,000 acres, far more than only the river.

Unexpectedly, the path before me, which began with an easily accessed trailhead from a good-sized parking lot, is deserted. In fact, it's quiet enough that not long into my hike I see a big doe ahead, casually crossing the trail. She stops to peer at me, so calm and unconcerned by my presence that her tail points downward, a sure sign of her relaxed state. I grin at her and she ambles off through the foliage, which in this first week of October is beginning to blaze with fall's vibrant colors.

I'm in the northern end of the park, home to the Lower New River. (This quirky waterway, said to be one of the oldest rivers on the planet, flows south to north rather than humdrum north to south.) Corseted by a tall, tight gorge that funnels the flowing river into raging rapids, the Lower New is also blessed with sandstone cliffs that soar upward from its banks.

Here, visitors will find world-class rock climbing, whitewater rafting and mountain biking. Farther south, the gorge widens into something akin to a canyon, with calm waters offering

WORDS TO THE WISE

New River Gorge National Park is accommodating to adventurers of all experience levels. If you'd like to try your hand at climbing for the first time, consider embarking on one of New River Mountain Guides' half-day climbing trips for beginners. *newriverclimbing .com*

If horseback riding appeals, Cowboy Town, located 6 miles from the New River Gorge Bridge, specializes in family-friendly beginner and intermediate rides through acres of unspoiled private land. *horsebackride thenewriver.com*

And finally, if you're not up for tackling raging whitewater rapids, you can enjoy a more family-friendly rafting trip on the Upper New. *aceraft.com*

▼

The New River offers great fishing and stunning views.

gentler pleasures like fishing and family-friendly paddling of all sorts.

That's not to say it's all daredevil action on the Lower Gorge. There's a range of well-maintained hiking trails rated from easy to strenuous, some of them winding around the remains of the old coal mining towns that dotted this area a century ago.

I'm finding Long Point, which is about 3 miles total, to be a mostly flat, serene walk through a forest rich in pine, oak, poplar, hemlock, maple and beech. The trees arch over my head, shading me from the sun, their leaves glowing red here, yellow there. Closer to eye level, the rhododendron and mountain laurel, for which the state is famous, grow in great, glossy thickets. I consider how this land must also dazzle when spring arrives and the trees are in full bloom.

I've been to the New River Gorge before—the first time was more than a decade ago. Back then I led a far more sedentary life. I didn't hike or bike, raft or ride. But part of my job as a writer is to experience new things, so I decided to visit the Lower Gorge, packing all the outdoor activities I could into two busy days. I went horseback riding and zip-lining. I even soared across the sky as a passenger in a World War II-era biplane. It's not a stretch to say that no matter the adventure you wish to experience, chances are you'll find it somewhere in the Lower Gorge.

But the most memorable of all the activities was rafting the New's famed whitewater, which had swollen with spring snowpack melt into Class IV rapids. I was an utter disaster, falling twice into the raging water, even going

PAT & CHUCK BLACKLEY

so far as to get sucked under the raft, an exploit I imagine was similar to spending a cycle in a giant washing machine. But even as I bounced around in the boat, even as wave after icy wave slapped me square in the face, I grew only more ebullient. Rafting the New River down that impossibly rugged gorge was one of the most challenging and purely gratifying things I'd ever done. It—somehow—made an outdoors person out of me.

Over the years I've returned many times to the Lower New area around the little town of Fayetteville, which is considered the gateway to the gorge. I'd never before hiked Long Point Trail, though. On this journey, I walk down the well-worn path, wondering how I managed to miss it until now. Because after a short scramble down a rocky incline, I finally arrive at the point from which the trail takes its name. The large stone outcropping reaches into the gorge to provide a vista so beautiful my jaw drops in amazement.

Before me unspools the famed New River Gorge Bridge. At 876 feet tall, it's the country's third highest bridge— and at 3,030 feet long, the Western Hemisphere's longest steel bridge.

Every third Saturday in October, spectators flood the area to celebrate Bridge Day and watch fearless BASE jumpers leap from the bridge into the gorge. You'll find information about shuttles, tickets and activities for the largest single-day festival in West Virginia at *officialbridgeday.com*.

I marvel at this mighty but graceful structure straddling the dense foliage of the gorge. The leaves look spattered, as if by a careless painter's brush, with the fiery colors of autumn. Far below I can spot the New River, the waterway that changed my life. I want to applaud the sight, but instead I just whisper a word of congratulations. I can't think of a more deserving site for America's newest national park. ◗

▼
BASE jumpers leap from fixed objects—with parachutes, of course!

▼
Thoroughbreds graze on sweet green grass at a postcard-worthy Kentucky horse farm.

"Dear old world ... you are very lovely, and I am glad to be alive in you."

—LUCY MAUD MONTGOMERY

NORTHEAST

A double rainbow brightens the sky over Pine Island Bay.

STORY BY
PAULETTE ROY

MYSTIC COUNTRY

FOLLOW THE WATER INTO EASTERN CONNECTICUT AND ESCAPE TO CHARMING SEASIDE TOWNS, RUGGED FORESTS AND HISTORIC FARMS.

FOR MANY YEARS, my husband, Paul, and I sailed the Mystic River into eastern Connecticut's Mystic Country. Because our boat was moored in the town of Groton, we often explored the region before heading home to Massachusetts. Here you'll find seaside villages with plenty of attractions for every interest and country roads that wind through pastoral landscapes. Mystic Country is an ideal place for a weekend getaway.

As much as I love being on the water, it is always a treat to get on land and walk around the village of Mystic, which is actually part of two towns: Groton on the west and Stonington on the east. Situated on the river, Mystic is a picture-perfect place to meander about, watch the boats navigate under the bascule bridge or peruse the shops in Colonial-era buildings along Main Street.

After exploring downtown, I often pop into Mystic Pizza for a quick slice (movie buffs will remember that this pizzeria was made famous by the 1988 movie of the same name, starring a young Julia Roberts and Matt Damon in his film debut). Still, there's more to Mystic than heavenly slices. It's a dining destination where restaurants serve farm-to-table ingredients and fresh seafood.

When I'm in the mood for a longer, more elegant meal, the S&P Oyster Restaurant and Bar is my go-to. The view from the patio overlooking the river and its gliding boats can't be beat.

You won't need to stay landbound when in Mystic. From May through mid-October, you can easily get out on the water via the two-masted schooner Argia, which hosts half-day sails or sunset cruises along the river out to Fishers Island Sound. The coastal scenery is fantastic (you'll sail past a few lighthouses), and you can even try your hand at helping the crew hoist and trim the sails. Another option is to board the Mystic Seaport

Points of INTEREST

REST STOP

Olde Mistick Village offers visitors a unique open-air shopping experience. This re-created 18th-century New England village has more than 60 small shops, gift stores with hand-crafted goods and a wide selection of eateries. *oldemistickvillage .com*

NOT TO BE MISSED

The 19-acre Mystic Seaport Museum features a re-created New England coastal village, a working shipyard, a replica of the Brant Point Lighthouse and the Charles W. Morgan, the last American whaling ship. Plan to stay for a few hours, if not most of the day. *mysticseaport.org*

FUN FACT

The bascule bridge that spans the Mystic River is an engineering feat. Built in 1920, it includes two 285-ton counterweights that balance the bridge as it raises. In summer months, the bridge opens at 40 minutes past the hour or on demand to let vessels pass under it.

▼

S&P Oyster Restaurant and Bar serves up seafood and river views.

Museum's 1908 coal-fired wooden steamboat, Sabino.

Mystic offers even more to discover beyond downtown proper. Venture farther outside and explore the Mystic Aquarium, whose main draws include structured live-animal interactions and hands-on exhibits. The museum uses these exhibits to educate visitors and strengthen their understanding and commitment to conserving the marine environment. The museum also serves as a marine mammal rescue and rehabilitation center, and it conducts extensive research projects related to the ocean environment.

Because I love the journey as much as the destination, I like to drive north along the back roads to my home in Massachusetts. This route leads to a world drastically different from the coastal villages. Here, river views give way to verdant farmlands and forests.

Initially, open farmlands and rustic barns, many of which are painted the ubiquitous barn red, dot the landscape in the town of North Stonington. One view in particular catches my eye—that of Gypsy Woods Farm, where Gypsy Vanner horses peacefully graze in pastures near a big red barn.

The terrain becomes more wooded as I reach Pachaug State Forest, the largest in Connecticut. The forest's 26,477 acres of trees, hills, streams and ponds sprawl across six towns: Sterling, Preston, Griswold, Voluntown, North Stonington and Plainfield. The word "Pachaug" is derived from a Native American word meaning "bend in the river" and refers to its namesake, which winds for 9 miles through the surrounding forests.

Pachaug has two main areas for recreational activities: Chapman and Green Falls. Outdoor activities such as hiking, biking, horseback riding, camping, swimming, boating, fishing and hunting are the main attractions. Hikers and walkers with a diverse range of abilities can take advantage of the trails throughout the state forest, from the wheelchair-accessible Rhododendron Sanctuary Trail (it is especially brilliant when the flowers are blooming in June and July) to a moderately challenging hike up the Mount Misery Trail (the only real option for an overview of the surrounding landscape). Backpacking enthusiasts often dot the longer trails, such as the 24-mile Pachaug Trail from Pachaug Pond to Green Falls Pond.

Back on the road, I pass through more rural landscapes, reminding me of my family's long, leisurely Sunday afternoon drives through the quintessential New England towns of Canterbury, Brooklyn and Pomfret. More red barns, offset with flowering shrubs and trees, are plentiful on the outskirts of these communities, and small-town greens attest to the region's past. In Pomfret, the Pomfret School, a college preparatory boarding and day school established in 1894 and featuring grounds designed by the world-renowned landscape architect Frederick Law Olmsted, occupies much of the center of the town's Pomfret Street Historic District. A number of buildings on the school's picturesque 500-acre campus are listed in the National Register of Historic Places, and the ivy-covered stone walls of the Norman-style Clark Chapel, along with its exquisite stained-glass windows, always capture the attention of passersby with their beauty.

Eventually I must remind myself that weekends don't last forever and I have to go home. For the remainder of my journey, I reflect on the rich contrasts and picturesque beauty of eastern Connecticut and put Mystic Country on my revisit list. ◗

▼
Stonington's Old Lighthouse Museum boasts an 1840 stone beacon.

▼
The sun sets serenely behind the Delaware Breakwater East End Lighthouse in Cape Henlopen State Park.

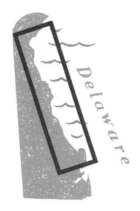

STORY BY
PAM GEORGE

BAYSHORE BYWAY

WITH VIEWS OF WATERWAYS AND RURAL FARMLAND, THIS SCENIC ROUTE IS A BLISSFUL BLAST FROM THE PAST.

I CAN'T PINPOINT the exact moment when I fell in love with Lewes, Delaware, the historic town that hugs the Delaware Bay and the Atlantic Ocean. All I know is that I found it impossible to resist the pull of its lighthouses, Colonial-era buildings, World War II observation towers and fine dining.

I wanted more from Lewes than a week's vacation could provide, so in 2013, my husband and I decided to purchase a condominium near the city limits. Since then, I've become familiar with the stretch of Interstate 95 and U.S. Route 1 that takes me from our home in Wilmington to the condo.

One day, when construction snarled I-95 traffic, I took Delaware Route 9, a two-lane scenic road that is part of the Delaware Bayshore Byway. Within minutes, I was cruising through open expanses of cornfields, moving past sun-dappled marshes and maneuvering hairpin turns just inches from the Delaware River.

I was immediately charmed and surprised. Connecting historic New Castle to the north and Lewes to the south, the byway offers many views that early settlers may have shared. You can easily visit both cities in one day. Birders, however, should take their time; the byway is along the Atlantic Flyway, and there are numerous vantage points.

Start by traveling south from New Castle, once the capital of the original Three Lower Counties of Pennsylvania. On June 15, 1776, a date now known and celebrated as Separation Day, colonists met at the courthouse to secede from both Pennsylvania and Britain. The architecture in New Castle ranges from the 17th-century Dutch House to red brick Georgians, such as the George Reed II House, and a three-story Gothic Revival home with a tower. And no daytrip is complete without pausing in Battery Park, a frequent festival site. It's so peaceful to sit on a bench under

REST STOPS

In New Castle, the staffers at Jessop's Tavern wear period costumes and serve fun fare such as New Sweden Meatloaf with lingonberry preserves, "Hutspot" Dutch Pot Roast and the Patriot Pulled Pork sandwich. *jessops-tavern.com*

In Lewes, book a stay at the trendy Dogfish Inn, which is owned by Dogfish Head Craft Brewery in the nearby town of Milton. *dogfish.com/inn*

NOT TO BE MISSED

Enjoy a guided tour of the New Castle Court House Museum, where in 1776 patriots declared their independence from Pennsylvania and Britain to form Delaware. *history .delaware.gov*

NEARBY ATTRACTION

The Junction and Breakwater Trail is a former rail line that links Lewes and Rehoboth Beach. *delawaregreenways .org*

▼

The New Castle Court House once served as Delaware's state capitol.

a leafy tree and watch cargo ships glide slowly to Philadelphia.

To the south, Delaware City rests along the Chesapeake & Delaware Canal. Locals come here eager to lift a mallet—several restaurants specialize in steamed crabs. The city is also the gateway to Fort Delaware State Park, a hulking fortress on Pea Patch Island in the Delaware River.

Step off the ferry and you're back in the 19th century, when the fort was a Union prison during the Civil War. The intimidating yet intriguing stone-and-brick structure is surrounded by a moat—despite the island location.

From the ramparts to the reeds, Fort Delaware is decidedly and delightfully remote. Tour the buildings or walk the Prison Camp Trail in search of ibises or the herons and egrets that nest here.

The American Birding Association's headquarters is located in Delaware City—and with good reason. It has easy access to the byway's two national wildlife refuges, a bit farther south.

Bombay Hook National Wildlife Refuge, in Smyrna, is a seasonal haven for 150,000 ducks and geese. Take a stroll on the beach, where shorebirds hunt for horseshoe crab eggs as deer and foxes pick their way through fields and woods. There is a 12-mile driving trail for a quick visit.

Closer to Lewes is Prime Hook Wildlife Refuge, which was established in 1963 following the Migratory Bird Conservation Act. More than 100,000 snow geese and 80,000 ducks pause here in the fall. Be sure to keep an eye out for nesting bald eagles, migrating peregrine falcons, egrets, herons and American bitterns.

Between the two refuges is DuPont Nature Center, which is dedicated to educating visitors about the ecological importance of Delaware Bay.

Back on Route 9 from Delaware City, enjoy the scenery as you drive. From the steeply pitched Reedy Point Bridge over the Chesapeake & Delaware Canal, you will see the Delaware River, as well as New Jersey, Maryland and, on a clear day, Philadelphia.

With no cars around for miles, you might slow down not only to manage a turn near a marsh but also to take in the view. The road often runs alongside rivers and creeks, particularly near Augustine Beach. (Avoid the byway if there have been heavy rains; flooding is common, and Route 9 has no shoulder.)

In summer, the road is framed by rows of cornstalks, which give way to farmhouses with wooden signs at the drive. Although the river is not visible, you can sense its proximity. Looming above the road is the skeletal Reedy Island Rear Range Lighthouse, even though there is no water in sight.

Watermen built the tiny towns of Leipsic and Little Creek with Route 9 as their main street. The homes' porches nearly touch the byway as it runs past fire halls and churches.

Route 9 comes to an end at the Dover Air Force Base near the John Dickinson Plantation. (Dickinson is called the Penman of the Revolution.) From here, it's about a half-hour trip to Lewes, founded in 1631 as a Dutch whaling colony. Today, the downtown district is a destination for history buffs, diners and leisurely shoppers.

Tour the Lewes Historical Society complex or visit Cape Henlopen State Park, where trails wind through scrubby pine forests and past Gordons Pond. Look for the concrete fire towers and other remnants of Fort Miles, the World War II Army base that used to occupy the land.

Relax on the park's ocean beach or head over to Lewes Beach to gaze out at the East End and Harbor of Refuge lighthouses. Book the 70-minute voyage on the Cape May–Lewes Ferry to Cape May, New Jersey, for a closer look.

Or, after a stay in Lewes, return north on the byway for a different angle on the route. There is something new to see every time. ●

Bird lovers flock to Prime Hook Wildlife Refuge to spot great egrets.

Mount Katahdin, Maine's highest peak, overlooks the Penobscot River.

STORY BY
HILARY NANGLE

HIGHLANDS

IN MAINE'S WILDERNESS WOODLANDS, HILARY NANGLE
DISCOVERS EASIER WAYS TO ROUGH IT.

WHENEVER I VENTURE inland from my coastal home to the woodlands north of Bangor, Maine, I'm awed by the region's raw beauty.

Here, in the Highlands, rugged mountains cradle pristine lakes and serene ponds. Tumbling waterways splash dense woodlands. Eagles soar and moose romp. The vast outdoor playground is laced with trails and blessed with an abundance of riches.

Let me tick off just a few highlights: 5,267-foot-high Mount Katahdin, which is Maine's highest peak, presides over the region. The 100-Mile Wilderness, considered the most arduous section of the 2,190-mile Appalachian Trail, shimmies through it. The Allagash Wilderness Waterway, a National Wild and Scenic River, flows northward from here. And Maine's largest lake, 117-acre Moosehead, is a mere drop in the Highlands' bucket.

Some come for paddling, hiking, boating and fishing; others for wildlife watching or artistic inspiration; and many simply to relax amid the wonders of one of Mother Nature's masterpieces.

You don't need to be a dedicated wilderness lover or to forgo creature comforts to delight in this region's many wonders.

Though unpaved roads (most owned by paper companies) web the forest, it's easier—and much kinder to your vehicle—to stick with the paved roads that skirt around it. So instead of trying to explore every nook, cranny and ridge of this humongous chunk of real estate, concentrate your efforts in one area.

Greenville, a frontier-like resort town, sits not only on the edge of Moosehead Lake and the 100-Mile Wilderness but also on the edge of civilization. East of here, pavement cedes to dirt. About 1,600 people reside in Greenville, making it the biggest city in these parts, although moose outnumber people three to one. You'll find restaurants and lodging here, as well as anything you might need before

REST STOP

After a day of outdoor fun at Moosehead Lake, sit down for a family-friendly dinner and enjoy the sunset and water view at Kelly's Landing in Greenville Junction.

FUN FACT

The Maine Highlands region goes big! It contains the state's tallest mountain (Katahdin), largest lake (Moosehead) and longest river (Penobscot).

WORDS TO THE WISE

Guiding has a long history in Maine. A Registered Maine Guide can help make your trip even more memorable, whether you're looking to kayak, hunt, fish, raft, hike or camp. *maineguides.org*

SIDE TRIP

Maine's third-most populous city, Bangor, offers a diverse array of attractions. Stop by Stephen King's house on West Broadway, test your luck at the Hollywood Casino, or admire modern and contemporary pieces at Zillman Art Museum.

▼

Baxter State Park teems with wildlife, including red foxes.

heading out into the wilderness, including Registered Maine Guides for fishing, hiking and wildlife safaris. Sharing Moosehead Lake's western shore are Greenville Junction and the village of Rockwood.

Boating is an essential mode of transportation here. During the early 20th century, more than 50 steamboats ferried tourists, delivered mail, carried cargo and towed acres-long log booms across the lake. Today, only one of them, which has been retrofitted with a diesel engine, remains in service as an excursion boat. Docked downtown at the Moosehead Maritime Museum, the Katahdin, dating from 1914 and locally called the Kate, is used for

narrated cruises on Moosehead Lake. On a fine day, you'll find no nicer way to spend a few hours soaking in the views and stories.

The distinctive cliff-faced peak at the lake's waist is Mount Kineo. In the early 20th century, a sprawling hotel with 425 rooms, a dining room and a 500-acre farm sat at its base. Today, only a few cottages and a nine-hole golf course remain, but Kineo's allure continues. Take the shuttle boat from the village dock in Rockwood to visit Kineo, walk the carriage paths along the shoreline or hike the moderate-to-strenuous trails ascending the peak.

Get an eagle's view of this vast, undeveloped region on a flightseeing tour aboard a floatplane. You'll be in awe of views of the lake, wilderness and distant Katahdin. Try Currier's Flying Service, operating here since 1982. The service also maintains a small aviation museum at its base in Greenville Junction.

In Greenville, the docents and staff in the Moosehead Historical Society's museums bring to life the region's history and heritage: the loggers, lumber barons, river drivers and rusticators (early tourists); the grand hotels and sporting camps; the train and steamship era; and the 1963 crash of a B-52 on a brutally cold winter day. Ask for directions to the wreckage-strewn memorial site on Elephant Mountain. If you go, be sure to treat the site respectfully.

The society's Outdoor Heritage Center, Eveleth-Crafts-Sheridan Historical House and Moosehead Lumbermen's Museum all share one campus. Take a drive to downtown Greenville to see the Moosehead Lake Aviation Museum and Center for Moosehead History, located in the same building.

The don't-blink village of Monson, about 15 miles south of Greenville, is known today as the southern entry to the 100-Mile Wilderness. Decades ago, however, it was renowned for its slate industry. (Black slate quarried and engraved here marks the gravesites of both John F. Kennedy and Jacqueline Kennedy Onassis.)

The legacy of the many immigrants who worked in the quarry lives on in the Finnish Farmers Club, which still holds traditional Finnish and contra dances, with instruction, from May through September. But if exploring the great outdoors is your passion, visit the Appalachian Trail Visitor Center for trail conditions, maps and info. Or, pop into the handful of shops and galleries in this increasingly artsy town hugging Lake Hebron.

▼

Hikers take on the Maine section of the Appalachian Trail.

▼

The grounds of the historic Blair Hill Inn boast 80 dazzling acres of gardens, woodlands and ponds.

▼

Boys splash in the waters of Moosehead Lake.

For a moderate day hike, pick up a picnic lunch at the Monson General Store and head to Borestone Mountain, a 1,600-acre Audubon Society preserve. The 2-mile trail to the summit rewards hikers with stunning panoramic views over Lake Onawa and the peaks that pepper the 100-Mile Wilderness.

You can ease into the wilderness at one of several traditional Maine sporting camps. Most are off the grid near a lake or pond and accessible via maintained roads through the woods.

Rates often include a private cabin, usually with a wood stove and gas lighting, and three hearty meals daily in a main lodge. Some of the cabins have plumbing, while others have a shared bathhouse. Swim, paddle, hike, fish or relax by day, and be sure to keep an eye out for wildlife, especially at dawn and dusk.

If you're looking to enjoy some trail hiking, Appalachian Mountain Club runs three trail-connected lodges in the 100-Mile Wilderness: Medawisla, Gorham Chairback and Little Lyford. Little Lyford lodge puts Gulf Hagas, nicknamed the Grand Canyon of the East, almost at your doorstep. Trails also link to West Branch Pond Camps, family owned and operated since 1910. Stay in one spot or hike between a few.

When pure darkness descends, the Maine wilderness often delivers a grand finale. Slip outside and enjoy the show, as stars glitter in inky skies and nature's symphony performs its moonlight serenade.

Let that music of the night inspire dreams reliving the day's events and anticipating many more to come—even if they occur while simply lazing about, immersed in the region's bounty. ●

▼
Fiery fall foliage puts on a show along Route 202 on the west side of Quabbin.

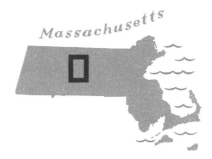

Massachusetts

STORY AND PHOTOS BY
PAUL REZENDES

QUABBIN RESERVOIR

MASSACHUSETTS BUILT QUABBIN RESERVOIR AS A WATER
SUPPLY AND GOT A SCENIC WONDER IN THE BARGAIN.

MASSACHUSETTS DIDN'T SET OUT to create one of New England's most beautiful wilderness areas when it dammed three branches of the Swift River back in the 1930s. It just worked out that way.

The state built Quabbin Reservoir to supply clean, reliable drinking water to the burgeoning population of the Boston metropolitan area 65 miles to the east. At the time, the plan to flood the Swift River Valley was fraught with controversy and heartache: It involved relocating hundreds of businesses and homes, more than 2,000 people and 6,000 graves.

When it finally filled to its capacity in 1946, Quabbin, which comes from the Nipmuck word for the meeting of many waters, was acclaimed as the world's biggest man-made reservoir. And it's still one of the largest in the United States, with a water storage capacity of 412 billion gallons, 39 square miles of surface area, 181 miles of shoreline and 60 islands.

Protected by forests on all sides to ensure water quality, Quabbin is often called "the accidental wilderness." The reservoir provides habitat for a wide variety of wildlife, including beavers, otters, bears, fishers, coyotes, moose, bobcats, wild turkeys and loons. Many anglers consider it one of the best freshwater fishing spots in southern New England.

I'm lucky enough to live near the north end of the Quabbin, and the area remains one of my favorite places to go out and shoot scenic photographs. The roads around the reservoir are rich with quaint New England towns, Colonial-style homes and picturesque white steepled churches.

Several abandoned roads trail off into the water toward the islands that used to be hilltop towns. One of these, on the west side of the reservoir on Route 202 in New Salem, offers one of my favorite overlooks. It's unmarked, so you have to watch closely as you travel south along Route 202 after its junction with

REST STOP

NEARBY ATTRACTIONS

Enjoy inviting farmsteads and elegant homes in nearby Hardwick.

Route 122. You'll find it on the left after passing the power line right-of-way. I especially like to visit in early morning or late evening, when low sun glints off the wooded hillsides or layers of fog flood the valley.

Enfield Lookout in Quabbin Park, which is off Route 9 at the south end of the reservoir in Belchertown, offers what is arguably the best view of the reservoir itself. A photographer's delight in any season, it's a winter favorite with bird-watchers hoping to spot the resident bald eagles. A small visitors center near the park entrance provides information and maps.

The east side of the reservation along Route 122 provides an excellent view at South Spectacle Pond in New Salem, with a primordial quality I simply can't resist. Farther south, Harvard Pond is a magical place replete with floating bogs, lily pads, small islands and insectivorous plants.

If you enjoy hiking, numbered gates provide easy access to several idyllic trails. One of the shortest hikes to the water is from Gate 35 at the end of Old North Dana Road off Route 122. After walking around the gate, bear left and hike straight south for good views of the reservoir and several islands.

At Gate 40, you can hike along the old road to Dana Common and find the remnants of old cellar holes and stone foundations. Gate 29 is another popular entrance, with a paved road lined with stately maple trees that's especially spectacular in autumn.

A longer hike to Rattlesnake Hill rewards you with a sweeping view of the reservoir from atop stone ledges. When I really want to get away from it all, I head for a peaceful hike along the east branch of the Swift River in Petersham. The river and forests here are pristine, and it's a great location for nature photography.

After 30 years and countless visits to the nooks and crannies of the Quabbin, I still look forward to each journey into this accidental wilderness. ☙

▼

The graceful Keystone Bridge was built by Adolphus Porter in 1866—with no mortar! It's easily accessible from Gate 30.

▼

The Mountaineer train arrives at Crawford Depot.

STORY BY
MARJORIE STEVENSON

WHITE MOUNTAINS

A FAMILY'S TRAIN TREK THROUGH NEW HAMPSHIRE'S
WHITE MOUNTAINS REVEALS THE BEST OF AUTUMN.

EVERY YEAR, rain or shine, our family takes the scenic route through the White Mountains of New Hampshire on a fall foliage trek.

We check the online foliage tracker sites early in the season to determine which dates and routes are the best to catch peak colors. We never tire of seeing the sunlit trees painting glorious hues of orange, red and yellow on the mountain peaks, or stopping at farm stands along the way for apple cider and other fall goodies.

Our trip takes us by way of Route 16 up to Conway, a quaint New England town where the people are friendly and welcoming. We then travel through the notches (mountain passes) and along the winding Kancamagus Highway.

Locally known as "the Kanc," it's often touted as one of the best fall foliage drives in the country.

Sometimes we deviate from our usual drive and book a fall foliage excursion aboard one of the historic trains of the Conway Scenic Railroad. Riding in the old trains is an experience I liken to traveling back in time.

The railway offers scenic excursions of various lengths (from 1 hour up to 8 hours) in beautifully restored trains, including the Dorothea Mae dome car, built in 1955, and the Gertrude Emma Pullman parlor car, built in 1898.

One of our favorite adventures was a dining excursion on the Mountaineer train. The five-hour trek included a three-course meal and snacks. On this

Points of INTEREST

To time your leaf peeping just right, check out the White Mountains Fall Foliage Tracker at *visitwhitemountains .com/foliage-tracker*.

In search of the perfect photo op? Have your camera ready to capture the Saco Valley and White Mountains ablaze in fall color from Cathedral Ledge in Cathedral Ledge State Park. Reach this iconic valley view by driving 1 mile to the top and taking a short hike to the scenic overlook.

NEARBY ATTRACTIONS

If you're traveling with kids, consider a trip to one of the nearby amusement parks. Santa's Village in Jefferson features fun rides, food and reindeer. Clark's Bears in Lincoln has a bear show, an acrobatic act, a train ride with the infamous wolfman, and a Victorian Main Street with lots of food and shops. Story Land in Glen offers attractions for little ones and their grown-ups.

▼

MaryEllen, Christopher and Logan ride the Dorthea Mae dome car.

trip, we arrived at the 1874 Victorian station—a historic destination in its own right—around 11 a.m., joined by our son, Christopher; his wife, MaryEllen; and our grandson Logan. With the conductor calling out "All Aboard!" the train departed the North Conway station, and our autumn adventure began.

The charismatic conductor shared stories about the old trains and the scenic vistas before us as we traveled through woodlands and crossed over aging trestles.

The round-trip train ride took us through Mount Washington Valley and over Crawford Notch (a deep, narrow mountain pass). Along the way, we saw deer grazing in a field and pebbled streams with crystal clear water. The views were absolutely breathtaking, especially from the Frankenstein Trestle, which was named for Godfrey Frankenstein, a German artist who spent time painting in this area in the 19th century.

As we chugged higher and higher through the notches, everything below us began to look small from our lofty perch—we felt as though we were floating on air.

The old train featured period wood-carved detailing and beautiful murals on the ceiling. The vintage decor was so ornate that it almost competed with the gorgeous view beyond the window for my attention.

People waved to welcome us as we arrived at our destination, the station at Crawford Notch. We stopped at the gift shop, where Logan got a bottle of bubbles and a stuffed goldfinch. He was so excited to find the songbird to add to his growing collection.

What better way is there to spend time with family than by taking an old-fashioned train ride? Traveling on historic railroad tracks—with the long, loud train whistle blowing—is one of the best ways I know to see the splendor of the White Mountains during fall foliage season. ◗

MARJORIE STEVENSON

STORY BY
MONICA ROERIG

MILLBROOK VILLAGE

PUT YOUR CARES AWAY AND BASK IN THE PAST AT
NEW JERSEY'S HISTORIC MILLBROOK VILLAGE.

VISITING HISTORIC MILLBROOK VILLAGE is an autumn tradition for our family.

Millbrook Village is in Hardwick, New Jersey, nestled along the banks of the Delaware River. Its story goes back to 1832, when a farmer named Abram Garis built a grain mill at the intersection of the area turnpike and a stream known as Van Campens Mill Brook. The village prospered until 1900, when the mill closed and folks left town.

Today, the historic village is part of the Delaware Water Gap National Recreation Area, administered by the National Park Service. It's not an exact replica of Garis' Millbrook, but it comes very close. In the 1960s, the Tocks Island Dam project prompted the re-creation of Millbrook Village. Some buildings were moved, while others were built on site. These structures include the grain mill; the blacksmith's barn; the post office; the church; the one-room schoolhouse; a few houses; and various sheds, barns and outbuildings.

▼

Shelves in the general store are lined with artifacts.

Points of INTEREST

FUN FACT

The Appalachian Trail runs more than 25 miles through Delaware Gap National Recreation Area. The trail crosses the Delaware River and the Delaware Water Gap on a walkway over the I-80 bridge.

SIDE TRIP

Delaware River Railroad Excursions takes passengers on a variety of fun trips, including rides on the Great Pumpkin Train and the Warren County Winery Train. Trips depart from the town of Phillipsburg. *877trainride.com*

NEARBY ATTRACTION

The Peters Valley Craft Fair takes place every fall and showcases works by more than 100 artists and artisans from across the United States. Jewelery, ceramics, fiber arts, metalwork and more are available to buy and admire. *petersvalley.org /events/craft-fair*

▼

Volunteers in period dress make apple butter with a paddled stirrer.

The brook still flourishes, and the once-bustling turnpike now serves as a scenic walking trail.

Every fall, the Millbrook Village Society, with the support of the National Park Service, hosts Millbrook Days, an annual event that brings the past into the present. Buildings are open to the public, and volunteers don period garb to re-enact the days of old. Some of my fondest childhood memories were made in this town.

On one particularly memorable fall visit, my mom, my brother, a few extended family members and I started our day in the wood shop admiring the craftsman at work and the array of wagon wheels and old tools. My mom warmed up by the potbellied wood stove while my grandfather chatted with the woodworker. I thought, *What was daily life like back then?* I couldn't imagine how difficult it must have been for average folks.

A chill in the air brought me back to the present, and I pulled my sweatshirt tighter around me. We walked along the stream until the sweet smell of apples caught our attention and led us to cider being pressed as it had been almost 150 years ago.

We made our way back into the small crowds of visitors to tour restored and replaced residential buildings. I felt as though I were walking into somebody's home. Every detail was so incredibly precise, from the hand-knit throws to the ornate furniture and delicate kitchenware. I could clearly envision the members of the family who had lived here going about their day.

Once outside, the bright sunshine and chilly October air welcomed us back into the village. We admired the skills of women who were spooling thread and dyeing yarn.

We passed a barn with an old tractor and soon found ourselves approaching the fully functioning grain mill. Inside the mill, the demonstrator ground away, producing bags of corn using a large, round flat stone powered by the creek. I looked around at the other visitors, whose eager, awestruck faces reflected my own state of amazement.

On our way back over the bridge, we paused to admire the picturesque white church, then followed a wooded path to the schoolhouse. Inside, my grandma recounted tales from her days of learning in a one-room schoolhouse, attracting the attention of some other visitors, who were eager to hear her wonderful stories. Smiling to myself, I couldn't imagine a place I'd rather be. I felt truly blessed to have this window to the past.

Now that I have a daughter of my own, I hope to carry on this tradition with my own little family. I am thankful to all the volunteers who contributed to preserving Millbrook and to those who have helped it endure. Their efforts allow people like me to experience the quiet essence of another time and make memories with people I love. ❦

Millbrook ◀
Days celebrates
old-fashioned arts,
such as grinding
and pressing
apples for cider.

▼
The gorge trail through Buttermilk Falls State Park passes several waterfalls as it descends 600 feet into the valley.

STORY AND PHOTOS BY
PAT & CHUCK BLACKLEY

FINGER LAKES

DELIGHT IN THE NATURAL BEAUTY, IDYLLIC PASTURES AND
MAJESTIC WATERFALLS OF NEW YORK'S FINGER LAKES.

THE FINGER LAKES awaken in spring with a telltale burst of light green buds in the vineyards, a rush of snowmelt over the many waterfalls and wildflowers awakening in the glens. Any season is beautiful here, but spring is our absolute favorite.

The region, located in rural western New York, is known for clear lakes, cascading waterfalls, fertile farm fields, historic places and small towns full of character and charm.

The region owes its landscape to the advance and retreat of glaciers, which over some time carved large, elongated holes in the ground that filled with water, forming 11 finger-shaped lakes. Those lakes are named Canadice, Canandaigua, Cayuga, Conesus,

Hemlock, Honeoye, Keuka, Otisco, Owasco, Seneca and Skaneateles.

Canadice is the shortest of the finger lakes, at just 3 miles, while Cayuga is the longest, at nearly 40 miles. Seneca is the deepest, at more than 630 feet. Beautiful to look at, these sky blue lakes are ideal for myriad summer adventures, including swimming, boating and fishing.

For thousands of years, the Iroquois Confederacy inhabited this area, and that influence endures—several of the lakes (and nearby towns) are named after Iroquois tribes, including the two largest lakes, Seneca and Cayuga.

The Finger Lakes region covers more than 9,000 square miles, with 650 miles of lake shoreline. It lies between the

NOT TO BE MISSED

The Finger Lakes' world-famous wine country is often compared to that of Germany's Rhine Valley. The wine trails of the Finger Lakes are popular with enthusiasts. The Cayuga Lake trail, the oldest in the nation, includes 16 wineries; Keuka Lake has eight; and Seneca Lake has 35. The wineries host festivals, wine and food pairings and many other events.

NEARBY ATTRACTIONS

Take a stroll, cast a line or watch a sunrise at the Canandaigua City Pier. The pier is lined with colorful rustic boathouses built in the 1850s—they're a popular attraction for photographers, tourists and artists.

The Women's Rights National Historical Park celebrates the first Women's Rights Convention, held in Seneca Falls in 1848. The park includes a visitor center, historic homes and the famed Wesleyan Chapel. *nps.gov/wori*

▼

A roadside stand near Locust Grove displays bright spring flowers.

large cities of Rochester and Syracuse and stretches southward to Elmira and Corning. In between, small villages and midsize towns form the heart of the area, with hundreds of motels, bed-and-breakfasts, restaurants, galleries, museums, parks and historic sites and landmarks.

The climate here, largely created by the lakes themselves, is ideal for growing grapes. Consequently, the Finger Lakes has become the largest and most famous wine-making area in the eastern United States, with more than 130 wineries spread along the lakes' shores. We love visiting the different wineries and soaking in the sublime beauty of the lakeside vineyards, a glass of Riesling or Pinot Noir pairing perfectly with the view.

Grapes are not the only crops that thrive in the fertile soils of this area. Oats, wheat, corn, apples, pears and many other fruits and vegetables are also grown throughout the region. One report notes that 1.47 million acres of land is dedicated to agriculture—the largest amount in the state. A thriving Amish and Mennonite population resides on picturesque farms, traveling these country roads in horse-drawn buggies. A drive through farmland in the Finger Lakes is a feast for the eyes, especially in spring when the fields are green, the fruit trees are blooming and fragrant, and calves are frolicking in the warm sunshine. Once harvesting starts, farmers markets and roadside stands beckon customers with fresh fruits and vegetables.

For us, the highlights of the Finger Lakes are Mother Nature's creations, carefully preserved in 26 state parks, many of which have campgrounds, beaches and thousands of miles of hiking and biking trails. The same glaciers that carved out deep, clear lakes also created spectacular, vast gorges and stunning waterfalls.

At state parks such as Taughannock Falls, Fillmore Glen, Watkins Glen, Robert H. Treman and Buttermilk Falls, scenic trails wind through these impressive gorges, passing tumbling falls, splashing cascades and unique geological formations. All the parks are at their best in spring, when the waterfalls are full and gushing and wildflowers are plentiful. We've spent many happy days exploring these breathtaking natural wonders.

While the larger cities in the Finger Lakes region have much to offer in the way of cultural attractions, we love to visit the smaller towns and rural villages to really absorb the flavor of the area. Just outside the popular Watkins Glen State Park, the village of Watkins Glen, at the southern tip of Seneca Lake, has much to offer. The village has an extensive history of car racing and is home to the Watkins Glen International Speedway, long known as the home of the Formula One United States Grand Prix, which it hosted for 20 years.

Downtown sidewalks and streets display murals and plaques that honor the cars and drivers of the Grand Prix. The International Motor Racing Research Center here is a great place to learn about the history of motor racing. Mornings and evenings find visitors and locals alike strolling along the village's lovely waterfront.

The village of Penn Yan, situated at the northern tip of Keuka Lake, was named for its early Pennsylvania (Penn) and Yankee (Yan) settlers. Besides a good selection of lodging and eateries,

▼

Taughannock Falls plunges 215 feet through a 400-foot gorge.

▼
The haunting call of a loon may break the silence of the sunrise over Keuka Lake.

▼
A lush lunch of spring greens is on the menu for these cows on a farm near Himrod.

the village has a variety of parks and shops. The Windmill Farm & Craft Market is famous for its impressive assortment of foods, quilts, crafts, antiques and Mennonite goods.

Horses and buggies are common sights here, as Mennonites and Amish from the outlying farms frequent the village. South of town, on the shores of beautiful Keuka Lake, we visited a handful of wineries along the Keuka Lake Wine Trail.

Many historical sites can be found in and around the town of Seneca Falls, which is believed to have been Frank Capra's inspiration for the village of Bedford Falls in his Christmas movie *It's a Wonderful Life*. This is where the first Women's Rights Convention was held in July of 1848, and the town is now home to the Women's Rights National Historical Park.

Also located here, the National Women's Hall of Fame explores the lives of famous American women such as Rachel Carson, Willa Cather and Bessie Coleman. Boaters on the Cayuga-Seneca Canal, which was constructed in the early 1800s to connect the Erie Canal to Cayuga Lake and Seneca Lake, add to the ambiance of the beautiful Canal Harbor, just off Main Street.

When we decided to visit the Finger Lakes for the first time years ago, we really didn't know what to expect. But the exquisite beauty of the lakes as well as the dramatic geology of the deep gorges and magnificent waterfalls left us awestruck. Add to that the pristine countryside and the friendly, laid-back charm of the small towns and villages, and we knew we had found an oasis we would return to time and again. ●

▼

Roughly 400 preserved cannons dot the Gettysburg battlefield.

STORY BY
JENNY WISNIEWSKI

GETTYSBURG

CIVIL WAR LORE COMES TO LIFE THROUGH THE PLACES AND
PEOPLE OF GETTYSBURG, PENNSYLVANIA.

OUR SUMMER DRIVE into Gettysburg followed in the footsteps of Confederate soldiers as they marched—nearly 160 years earlier—into what would be a pivotal battle in America's Civil War. Their journey, too, took place on a hot July day along what was then called Chambersburg Pike, one of 10 roads leading into Gettysburg. As John (my husband), Ryan (our son), Tilly (our dog) and I passed through southeastern Pennsylvania's countryside with its distinctive saltbox farmhouses, I could feel my curiosity growing about this place that I knew of only from my school history books.

Many of our friends and family had recommended that we stop to see the impressive 377-foot cyclorama at the Gettysburg National Military Park Museum and Visitor Center. The next day we were to learn that the cyclorama's positive reviews held true—and that there was much more to see and discover in Gettysburg.

At the aptly named Battlefield Bed and Breakfast Inn, a friendly innkeeper greeted us and led us on a short tour of the 1809 house, which was once owned by the abolitionists Cornelius and Anna Houghtelin and used by Brigadier General Wesley Merritt as his headquarters during the battle. The narrow staircase, wide-planked floors, ornate fireplace and deep-set window bays reminded us of the history we were intimately inhabiting.

A small display case hanging on the wall of what was once the original parlor held the preserved detritus of battle—buttons, buckles and military insignia—all found by visitors on the 30-acre property. I was feeling fully immersed in Civil War history even before listening to our breakfast presentation, a ritual at the inn.

Dressed as a Union soldier, Mike, a retired Gettysburg National Military Park Museum curator, told stories of valor and suffering, drawing the war's

Ghost tours abound in Gettysburg. If you love a good ghost story, check out Ghostly Images of Gettysburg or one of the Historic Farnsworth House Inn's ghost tours. *gettysburgbattle fieldtours.com* and *farnsworthhouseinn .com*

The guided 8 Miles from Slavery Tour highlights the stories of Gettysburg's large Black community in the years leading up to the Civil War. *gbltg.com*

FUN FACT

The president we usually associate with Gettysburg is Abraham Lincoln, but another famed president, Dwight D. Eisenhower, built his home and farm on 189 acres in this bucolic setting. It is now preserved as the Eisenhower National Historic Site. *nps.gov/eise*

NEARBY ATTRACTION

The Jennie Wade House Museum honors the life of Jennie Wade, the sole civilian killed during the battle. *facebook.com /jenniewadehouse*

▼

An immersive cyclorama depicts the events of Pickett's Charge.

outlines as we sipped hot coffee with our country breakfast.

As we toured the vast battlefield, I found the preservation of some details and the re-creation of others awe inspiring. I felt keenly attached to history.

With our licensed guide, Fred, leading the way in his sedan, the four of us followed close behind during the three-hour, pandemic-safe tour. The drive to our first point of interest gave us a feel for the expanse of Gettysburg. The National Military Park sits on nearly 6,000 acres of land with more

than 26 miles of road connecting the various sites. Fred pointed out the memorial commissioned by our home state to honor its veterans—one of 30 state-commissioned memorials. More than 1,300 monuments and memorials honoring soldiers exist in the park, along with about 400 cannons.

We soon arrived at what had once been a peach orchard, listening as Fred explained that because bullets rocketed through the air from so many different directions in this area, later, bullets that had fused together midair were found lying on the ground.

A monument dedicated to General Winfield Scott Hancock overlooks Gettysburg National Military Park.

▼

A colorful summer sunset is captured from Little Round Top hill.

At the portentously named Cemetery Ridge—our final stop—we stood on the high ground where Union forces had held a defensive position. We reflected on the site of Pickett's Charge and the Confederate Army's last gasp.

Although the town of Gettysburg revolves around its history, it's also got plenty of modern life. The town has more than 7,600 residents, the 189-year-old Gettysburg College and a thriving restaurant scene.

We began with a comforting dinner at Dobbin House Tavern. Although dinner is served in seven historic rooms, we chose to sit outside under a large tent, a soft summer breeze keeping us cool and social distancing keeping us safe.

The restaurant had once served as a Civil War hospital, and I had to wonder, Did every place around here serve as a Civil War hospital? Given that at least 7,000 soldiers died on the battlefield, that might not be far from the truth.

The musty scent of timeworn wood hit us as we walked through the door of the old house. As we made our way up a winding staircase, we noticed intricately handcarved woodwork and paused to peer into a preserved crawl space that was once used to hide fugitive slaves who were escaping on the Underground Railroad.

The cellar, now the restaurant's pub, transported us back to Revolutionary America. (The house was actually built in 1776.) The room-length bar, the waitresses dressed as barmaids in period garb, and the wooden booths were illuminated only by lanterns.

We ended our trip with a walk down Baltimore Street, where clusters of people waited for one of Gettysburg's many ghost tours.

Though the battlefield's bloodstains are long buried, Civil War lore lives on, and Gettysburg's descendants remain committed to telling it. For this, I felt grateful. ●

STORY BY
KAITLIN STAINBROOK

TRUSTOM POND WILDLIFE REFUGE

NEARLY 800 ACRES OF WILDLIFE HABITATS AND 300 SPECIES OF BIRDS AWAIT VISITORS TO THIS SCENIC REFUGE.

IT WOULD BE HARD to walk away from the Trustom Pond National Wildlife Refuge without becoming more of a bird expert, thanks to the knowledgeable volunteer staff at the visitors center, plus the detailed interpretive panels scattered throughout the three miles of nature trails and four viewing platforms. Centered around the only undeveloped coastal salt pond in Rhode Island, this refuge is an important habitat for 300 bird species. Look for least terns and piping plovers, which make use of the barrier beach as a nesting site.

On the pond itself, you'll have the chance to spot 30-plus varieties of waterfowl, including ruddy ducks. (Check in with one of the volunteers to get the scoop on any recently spotted species.) As you meander through the refuge, trust me—it will begin to feel like your natural habitat, too. ◗

Piping plovers and least terns (like the one above) nest on the beach.

KENNETH CANNING/ISTOCK.COM

▼

The rolling hills and scenic views of the Mad River Valley make taking great photos easy.

STORY BY
DANA FREEMAN

MAD RIVER VALLEY

DANA FREEMAN SAVORS THE MANY DELIGHTS OF VERMONT'S MAD RIVER VALLEY.

FOR YEARS, Saturdays in my house meant a trip to the Mad River Valley for my children's weekly ski program at the Sugarbush Resort. As I made the early morning trek along Route 100, I was so concerned with getting my kids to their lessons on time that I rarely took time to enjoy the incredible beauty of the valley and, frankly, took it for granted.

I would whiz by boutique shops and restaurants in towns like Waterbury and Waitsfield and think about how, some day, I'd make time to explore this idyllic place on the east side of Vermont's Green Mountains. In the years since my kids have grown, I've regularly returned to the Mad River Valley and experienced it at a much more leisurely pace and through a different and unhurried lens.

With rolling hills, gentle curves and scenic vistas, Vermont's Route 100 is aptly considered to be one of the most picturesque drives in New England. While I haven't driven all 146 miles of the byway, I can tell you that the stretch between Waitsfield and Warren is not only stunning but also offers a rich abundance of things to see and do along the journey.

If, like me, you are a sucker for covered bridges, then you are in luck. Vermont has more than 100 of them, and you can see three of them on a short loop that starts and ends at the Mad River Chamber of Commerce in Waitsfield (handy if you need a map or more information). Right outside of the parking lot, you will find the Great Eddy Covered Bridge, also known as

Points of INTEREST

REST STOP

The quirky rooms at the Pitcher Inn each embody a unique Vermont theme. The School Room, for example, is modeled after a Vermont one-room schoolhouse. The inn has two restaurants that are open to the public, including Tracks, an indoor/outdoor pub. *pitcherinn.com*

NOT TO BE MISSED

Vermont is known as the home of Ben & Jerry's ice cream, but Vermonters will tell you that you cannot visit without trying a creemee (aka soft serve ice cream). Head to Canteen Creemee Co. and order the Bad Larry (maple ice cream drizzled in maple goodness). *canteencreemee.com*

SIDE TRIP

Accommodating riders of all levels, the Icelandic Horse Farm in Fayston offers trail rides and multiday treks throughout the area. Even if you don't ride, you are welcome to visit the farm to see the horses. *icelandichorses.com*

▼

The Joslin Round Barn houses the Green Mountain Cultural Center.

the Waitsfield Covered Bridge. Built in 1833, it is the oldest operating covered bridge in Vermont.

To find the Pine Brook Covered Bridge, head north on Route 100, make a left onto Tremblay Road and then a slight detour north on North Road. Also known as the Wilder Covered Bridge, the Pine Brook bridge dates back to 1855 and is still intact and fully operational.

Next, wend your way south past Waitsfield Common, and you will come upon the family owned and operated von Trapp Farmstead—an absolute must for cheese lovers. Be

sure to sample the washed-rind Oma (a silver medalist of the World Cheese Awards) and the natural-rind Mad River Blue (a two-time winner of the Good Food Awards).

To see the last covered bridge in the area, located in Warren Village, drive south. The views of Mount Ellen along this part of Common Road are simply magnificent. About 2 miles before you arrive at the Warren Covered Bridge, make a quick pit stop for lunch, a snack or a cold drink at the East Warren Community Market.

Vermont is an outdoor playground. A walk along any section of the Mad

River Path is a fantastic way to explore the valley on foot. This wide network of meandering public pathways connects the surrounding communities with trails that range in difficulty from easy to strenuous.

If you aren't up for a hike, walk the 1.2-mile West Greenway path. You'll find the trailhead in the parking lot off Meadow Road, just below Route 100. Follow the dirt trail as it winds its way alongside the Mad River, ending across from the 1824 House, an excellent spot for a sandwich. If you want to get in the river, the Silver Trout in Waitsfield offers fly-fishing lessons and excellent guided tours.

Another short but rewarding walk I like to take is the half-mile Waitsfield Country Roads loop. It has lush views of the Green Mountains and passes by the lovingly restored Skinner Barn, which dates back to 1891 and sits on a former dairy farm.

Nestled in the heart of the Green Mountains, Blueberry Lake is another hidden gem. One of the most gorgeous outdoor spaces in the valley, it offers beginner and intermediate hiking trails, plus a swimming area.

Not only do we have an impressive number of talented local artists in Vermont, we also have organizations like Mad River Valley Arts that support and showcase them through carefully curated art shows, workshops and other events.

Aside from the art galleries sprinkled about the towns, there is a full lineup of fairs, festivals and shows from July through early fall. One of my favorites is the Mad River Valley Craft Fair in Waitsfield. The fair celebrated its 50th anniversary on Labor Day weekend of 2021; the celebration featured more than 100 juried artists, live music, artist demos and samples of made-in-Vermont foods and beverages.

For more locally produced goods, check out the Waitsfield Farmers

▼
Autumn transforms the valley.

▼

A double rainbow spans the sky in Waitsfield after an August rain.

▼

The Trapp Family Lodge in Stowe welcomes hikers, skiers and other guests all year long.

Market, which takes place on the town green every Saturday from mid-May to mid-October. It is one of the largest and most popular markets in the state and is a total experience. I like to arrive early to grab a pastry from Red Hen Baking Co. and peruse the stalls while listening to live music. You will find stands with local produce, cut flowers, prepared foods and handmade goods to gift or treasure.

There are a number of quirky places unique to the Mad River Valley that are also worthy of a visit. When my kids were little, we frequently went to the Big Picture Cafe because it's one part diner, one part beer garden and one part movie theater. The cafe is famous for its Very Small Donuts, which are available on Friday, Saturday and Sunday mornings. You cannot leave Vermont without having at least one of these maple-glazed treats.

The Knoll Farm is another all-in-one attraction. With nationally recognized historic buildings, this family-owned farm raises Icelandic sheep, has a yarn shop featuring small-flock yarns, grows eight varieties of organic blueberries (ripe and ready for picking mid-July through August) and has a retreat center known as the Refuge. You can purchase a day pass that lets you pick your own berries, visit the sheep and explore miles of hiking trails. The Farm Store sells convenient premade picnic baskets with a full spread of edible delights: cheeses, salami, fruit, chutneys and chocolate.

I feel incredibly fortunate to live near the Mad River Valley, and I make it a habit to visit this thriving community. ✿

"**Maine, because of its singular and profound beauty, is a place of worship without walls. I love it so.**"

—MAY DAVIDSON, *WHATEVER IT TAKES*

▼

The still waters of Mathews Cove at Lily Bay State Park reflect a gorgeous Maine sunset.